FALSEHOOD IN WAR-TIME

CONTAINING AN ASSORTMENT OF LIES CIRCULATED
THROUGHOUT THE NATIONS DURING
THE GREAT WAR

BY

ARTHUR PONSONBY, M.P.

NEW YORK
E. P. DUTTON & CO., Inc.

PREFACE

In compiling and collecting material for this volume, I am indebted to Lord Tavistock for his sympathetic help and useful suggestions. Professor Salvemini, Mr. Francis Nielson, Mr. T. Dixon, Mrs. C. R. Buxton, Mrs. Urie, Miss Durham, and Mrs. Wallis have also assisted me with contributions and in making investigations. My thanks are due to various correspondents who have furnished me with material. I am specially grateful to Miss Margaret Digby for her research work and for the revision of the proofs.

A. P.

CONTENTS

"A lie never lives to be old."

SOPHOCLES.

"When war is declared, Truth is the first casualty."

"Kommt der Krieg ins Land
Gibt Lügen wie Sand."

"You will find wars are supported by a class of argument which, after the war is over, the people find were arguments they should never have listened to."

JOHN BRIGHT.

"In the arena of international rivalry and conflict men have placed patriotism above truthfulness as the indispensable virtue of statesmen."

STANLEY BALDWIN.

"It is easier to make money by lies than by truth. Truth has only one power, it can kindle souls. But, after all, a soul is a greater force than a crowd."

G. LOWES DICKINSON.

"And when war did come we told youth, who had to get us out of it, tall tales of what it really is and of the clover-beds to which it leads."

J. M. BARRIE.

FALSEHOOD IN WAR-TIME

INTRODUCTION

THE object of this volume is not to cast fresh blame on authorities and individuals, nor is it to expose one nation more than another to accusations of deceit.

Falsehood is a recognized and extremely useful weapon in warfare, and every country uses it quite deliberately to deceive its own people, to attract neutrals, and to mislead the enemy. The ignorant and innocent masses in each country are unaware at the time that they are being misled, and when it is all over only here and there are the falsehoods discovered and exposed. As it is all past history and the desired effect has been produced by the stories and statements, no one troubles to investigate the facts and establish the truth.

Lying, as we all know, does not take place only in war-time. Man, it has been said, is not "a veridical animal," but his habit of lying is not nearly so extraordinary as his amazing readiness to believe. It is, indeed, because of human credulity that lies flourish. But in war-time the authoritative organization of lying is not sufficiently recognized. The deception of whole peoples is not a matter which can be lightly regarded.

A useful purpose can therefore be served in the interval of so-called peace by a warning which people can examine with dispassionate calm, that the authorities in each country do, and indeed must, resort to this practice in order, first, to justify themselves by depicting the enemy as an undiluted criminal; and secondly, to inflame popular passion sufficiently to secure recruits for the continuance of the struggle.   They cannot afford to tell the truth.   In some cases it must be admitted that at the moment they do not know what the truth is.

The psychological factor in war is just as important as the military factor.   The *morale* of civilians, as well as of soldiers, must be kept up to the mark.   The War Offices, Admiralties, and Air Ministries look after the military side.   Departments have to be created to see to the psychological side.   People must never be allowed to become despondent; so victories must be exaggerated and defeats, if not concealed, at any rate minimized, and the stimulus of indignation, horror, and hatred must be assiduously and continuously pumped into the public mind by means of "propaganda."   As Mr. Bonar Law said in an interview to the United Press of America, referring to patriotism, "It is well to have it properly stirred by German frightfulness"; and a sort of general confirmation of atrocities is given by vague phrases which avoid responsibility for the authenticity of any particular story, as when Mr. Asquith said (*House of Commons, April* 27, 1915): "We shall not forget this horrible record of calculated cruelty and crime."

The use of the weapon of falsehood is more necessary in a country where military conscription is not the law of the land than in countries where the manhood of the nation is automatically drafted into the Army, Navy, or Air Service.   The public can be worked up emotionally by sham ideals.   A sort of collective hysteria spreads and rises until finally it gets the better of sober people and reputable newspapers.

With a warning before them, the common people

may be more on their guard when the war cloud next appears on the horizon and less disposed to accept as truth the rumours, explanations, and pronouncements issued for their consumption. They should realize that a Government which has decided on embarking on the hazardous and terrible enterprise of war must at the outset present a one-sided case in justification of its action, and cannot afford to admit in any particular whatever the smallest degree of right or reason on the part of the people it has made up its mind to fight. Facts must be distorted, relevant circumstances concealed, and a picture presented which by its crude colouring will persuade the ignorant people that their Government is blameless, their cause is righteous, and that the indisputable wickedness of the enemy has been proved beyond question. A moment's reflection would tell any reasonable person that such obvious bias cannot possibly represent the truth. But the moment's reflection is not allowed; lies are circulated with great rapidity. The unthinking mass accept them and by their excitement sway the rest. The amount of rubbish and humbug that pass under the name of patriotism in war-time in all countries is sufficient to make decent people blush when they are subsequently disillusioned.

At the outset the solemn asseverations of monarchs and leading statesmen in each nation that they did not want war must be placed on a par with the declarations of men who pour paraffin about a house knowing they are continually striking matches and yet assert they do not want a conflagration. This form of self-deception, which involves the deception of others, is fundamentally dishonest.

War being established as a recognized institution to be resorted to when Governments quarrel, the people are more or less prepared. They quite willingly delude themselves in order to justify their own actions. They are anxious to find an excuse for displaying their patriotism, or they are disposed to seize the opportunity for the excitement and new life of adventure which war opens out to them. So there is a sort of national wink, everyone goes forward, and the individual, in his turn, takes up lying as a patriotic duty. In the low standard of morality which prevails in war-time, such a practice appears almost innocent. His efforts are sometimes a little crude, but he does his best to follow the example set. Agents are employed by authority and encouraged in so-called propaganda work. The type which came prominently to the front in the broad-casting of falsehood at recruiting meetings is now well known. The fate which overtook at least one of the most popular of them in England exemplifies the depth of degradation to which public opinion sinks in a war atmosphere.

With eavesdroppers, letter-openers, decipherers, tele-phone tappers, spies, an intercept department, a forgery department, a criminal investigation department, a pro-paganda department, an intelligence department, a censorship department, a ministry of information, a Press bureau, etc., the various Governments were well equipped to " instruct " their peoples.

The British official propaganda department at Crewe House, under Lord Northcliffe, was highly successful. Their methods, more especially the raining down of millions of leaflets on to the German Army, far sur-passed anything undertaken by the enemy. In *The Secrets of Crewe House*,[1] the methods are described for our satisfaction and approval. The declaration that

[1] *The Secrets of Crewe House*, Sir Campbell Stuart, K.B.E.

only " truthful statements " were used is repeated just too often, and does not quite tally with the description of the faked letters (page 99) and bogus titles and book-covers (page 104), of which use was made. But, of course, we know that such clever propagandists are equally clever in dealing with us after the event as in dealing with the enemy at the time. In the apparently candid description of their activities we know we are hearing only part of the story. The circulators of base metal know how to use the right amount of alloy for us as well as for the enemy.

In the many tributes to the success of British propaganda from German Generals and the German Press, there is no evidence that our statements were always strictly truthful. To quote one : General von Hutier, of the Sixth German Army, sent a message (page 115), in which the following passage occurs :

The method of Northcliffe at the Front is to distribute through airmen a constantly increasing number of leaflets and pamphlets ; the letters of German prisoners are falsified in the most outrageous way ; tracts and pamphlets are concocted, to which the names of German poets, writers, and statesmen are forged, or which present the appearance of having been printed in Germany, and bear, for example, the title of the Reclam series, when they really come from the Northcliffe press, which is working day and night for this same purpose. His thought and aim are that these forgeries, however obvious they may appear to the man who thinks twice, may suggest a doubt, even for a moment, in the minds of those who do not think for themselves, and that their confidence in their leaders, in their own strength, and in the inexhaustible resources of Germany may be shattered.

The propaganda, to begin with, was founded on the shifting sand of the myth of Germany's *sole* responsi-

bility.[1] Later it became slightly confused owing to the
inability of our statesmen to declare what our aims
were, and towards the end it was fortified by descriptions of the magnificent, just, and righteous peace
which was going to be " established on lasting foundations." This unfortunately proved to be the greatest
falsehood of all.

In calm retrospect we can appreciate better the disastrous effects of the poison of falsehood, whether
officially, semi-officially, or privately manufactured. It
has been rightly said that the injection of the poison of
hatred into men's minds by means of falsehood is a
greater evil in war-time than the actual loss of life.
The defilement of the human soul is worse than the
destruction of the human body. A fuller realization of
this is essential.

Another effect of the continual appearance of false
and biased statement and the absorption of the lie
atmosphere is that deeds of real valour, heroism, and
physical endurance and genuine cases of inevitable
torture and suffering are contaminated and desecrated;
the wonderful comradeship of the battlefield becomes
almost polluted. Lying tongues cannot speak of
deeds of sacrifice to show their beauty or value. So it
is that the praise bestowed on heroism by Government
and Press always jars, more especially when, as is
generally the case with the latter, it is accompanied by
cheap and vulgar sentimentality. That is why one
instinctively wishes the real heroes to remain unre-
cognized, so that their record may not be smirched by
cynical tongues and pens so well versed in falsehood.

When war reaches such dimensions as to involve
the whole nation, and when the people at its conclusion

[1] See page 57.

find they have gained nothing but only observe wide-spread calamity around them, they are inclined to become more sceptical and desire to investigate the foundations of the arguments which inspired their patriotism, inflamed their passions, and prepared them to offer the supreme sacrifice. They are curious to know why the ostensible objects for which they fought have none of them been attained, more especially if they are the victors. They are inclined to believe, with Lord Fisher, that " The nation was fooled into the war " (" *London Magazine*," *January* 1920). They begin to wonder whether it does not rest with them to make one saying true of which they heard so much, that it was " a war to end war."

When the generation that has known war is still alive, it is well that they should be given chapter and verse with regard to some of the best-known cries, catchwords, and exhortations by which they were so greatly influenced. As a warning, therefore, this collection is made. It constitutes only the exposure of a few samples. To cover the whole ground would be impossible. There must have been more deliberate lying in the world from 1914 to 1918 than in any other period of the world's history.

There are several different sorts of disguises which falsehood can take. There is the deliberate official lie, issued either to delude the people at home or to mislead the enemy abroad ; of this, several instances are given. As a Frenchman has said : " Tant que les peuples seront armés, les uns contre les autres, ils auront des hommes d'état menteurs, comme ils auront des canons et des mitrailleuses." (" As long as the peoples are armed against each other, there will be lying statesmen, just as there will be cannons and machine guns.")

A circular was issued by the War Office inviting reports on war incidents from officers with regard to the enemy and stating that strict accuracy was not essential so long as there was inherent probability.

There is the deliberate lie concocted by an ingenious mind which may only reach a small circle, but which, if sufficiently graphic and picturesque, may be caught up and spread broadcast; and there is the hysterical hallucination on the part of weak-minded individuals.

There is the lie heard and not denied, although lacking in evidence, and then repeated or allowed to circulate.

There is the mistranslation, occasionally originating in a genuine mistake, but more often deliberate. Two minor instances of this may be given.

The Times (agony column), July 9, 1915 :

JACK F. G.—If you are not in khaki by the 20th, I shall cut you dead.—ETHEL M.

The Berlin correspondent of the *Cologne Gazette* transmitted this :

If you are not in khaki by the 20th, *hacke ich dich zu Tode* (I will hack you to death).

During the blockade of Germany, it was suggested that the diseases from which children suffered had been called *Die englische Krankheit*, as a permanent reflection on English inhumanity. As a matter of fact, *die englische Krankheit* is, and always has been, the common German name for rickets.

There is the general obsession, started by rumour and magnified by repetition and elaborated by hysteria, which at last gains general acceptance.

There is the deliberate forgery which has to be very

carefully manufactured but serves its purpose at the moment, even though it be eventually exposed.

There is the omission of passages from official documents of which only a few of the many instances are given ;[1] and the " correctness " of words and commas in parliamentary answers which conceal evasions of the truth.

There is deliberate exaggeration, such, for instance, as the reports of the destruction of Louvain : " The intellectual metropolis of the Low Countries since the fifteenth century is now no more than a heap of ashes " (*Press Bureau, August* 29, 1914), " Louvain has ceased to exist " (" *The Times,*" *August* 29, 1914). As a matter of fact, it was estimated that about an eighth of the town had suffered.

There is the concealment of truth, which has to be resorted to so as to prevent anything to the credit of the enemy reaching the public. A war correspondent who mentioned some chivalrous act that a German had done to an Englishman during an action received a rebuking telegram from his employer : " Don't want to hear about any good Germans " ; and Sir Philip Gibbs, in *Realities of War*, says : " At the close of the day the Germans acted with chivalry, which I was not allowed to tell at the time."

There is the faked photograph ("the camera cannot lie ").[2] These were more popular in France than here. In Vienna an enterprising firm supplied atrocity photographs with blanks for the headings so that they might be used for propaganda purposes by either side.

The cinema also played a very important part, especially in neutral countries, and helped considerably in turning opinion in America in favour of coming in on

[1] See page 140.   [2] See page 135.

the side of the Allies. To this day in this country attempts are made by means of films to keep the wound raw.

There is the " Russian scandal," the best instance of which during the war, curiously enough, was the rumour of the passage of Russian troops through Britain.[1] Some trivial and imperfectly understood statement of fact becomes magnified into enormous proportions by constant repetition from one person to another.

Atrocity lies were the most popular of all, especially in this country and America ; no war can be without them. Slander of the enemy is esteemed a patriotic duty. An English soldier wrote (" *The Times,*" *September* 15, 1914): " The stories in our papers are only exceptions. There are people like them in every army." But at the earliest possible moment stories of the maltreatment of prisoners have to be circulated deliberately in order to prevent surrenders. This is done, of course, on both sides. Whereas naturally each side tries to treat its prisoners as well as possible so as to attract others.

The repetition of a single instance of cruelty and its exaggeration can be distorted into a prevailing habit on the part of the enemy. Unconsciously each one passes it on with trimmings and yet tries to persuade himself that he is speaking the truth.

There are lies emanating from the inherent unreliability and fallibility of human testimony. No two people can relate the occurrence of a street accident so as to make the two stories tally. When bias and emotion are introduced, human testimony becomes quite valueless. In war-time such testimony is accepted as

[1] See page 63.

conclusive. The scrappiest and most unreliable evidence is sufficient—" the friend of the brother of a man who was killed," or, as a German investigator of his own liars puts it, "somebody who had seen it," or, "an extremely respectable old woman."

There is pure romance. Letters of soldiers who whiled away the days and weeks of intolerable waiting by writing home sometimes contained thrilling descriptions of engagements and adventures which had never occurred.

There are evasions, concealments, and half-truths which are more subtly misleading and gradually become a governmental habit.

There is official secrecy which must necessarily mislead public opinion. For instance, a popular English author, who was perhaps better informed than the majority of the public, wrote a letter to an American author, which was reproduced in the Press on May 21, 1918, stating :

There are no Secret Treaties of any kind in which this country is concerned. It has been publicly and clearly stated more than once by our Foreign Minister, and apart from honour it would be political suicide for any British official to make a false statement of the kind.

Yet a series of Secret Treaties existed. It is only fair to say that the author, not the Foreign Secretary, is the liar here. Nevertheless the official pamphlet, *The Truth about the Secret Treaties*, compiled by Mr. McCurdy, was published with a number of *unacknowledged excisions*, and both Lord Robert Cecil in 1917 and Mr. Lloyd George in 1918 declared (the latter to a deputation from the Trade Union Congress) that our policy was not directed to the disruption of Austro-Hungary, although they both knew that under the Secret Treaty concluded with Italy in April

1915 portions of Austria-Hungary were to be handed over to Italy and she was to be cut off from the sea. Secret Treaties naturally involve constant denials of the truth.

There is sham official indignation depending on genuine popular indignation which is a form of falsehood sometimes resorted to in an unguarded moment and subsequently regretted. The first use of gas by the Germans and the submarine warfare are good instances of this.[1]

Contempt for the enemy, if illustrated, can prove to be an unwise form of falsehood. There was a time when German soldiers were popularly represented cringing, with their arms in the air and crying " Kamerad," until it occurred to Press and propaganda authorities that people were asking why, if this was the sort of material we were fighting against, had we not wiped them off the field in a few weeks.

There are personal accusations and false charges made in a prejudiced war atmosphere to discredit persons who refuse to adopt the orthodox attitude towards war.

There are lying recriminations between one country and another. For instance, the Germans were accused of having engineered the Armenian massacres, and they, on their side, declared the Armenians, stimulated by the Russians, had killed 150,000 Mohammedans (*Germania*, *October* 9, 1915).

Other varieties of falsehood more subtle and elusive might be found, but the above pretty well cover the ground.

A good deal depends on the quality of the lie. You must have intellectual lies for intellectual people and crude lies for popular consumption, but if your popular

[1] See page 146.

lies are too blatant and your more intellectual section are shocked and see through them, they may (and indeed they did) begin to be suspicious as to whether they were not being hoodwinked too. Nevertheless, the inmates of colleges are just as credulous as the inmates of the slums.

Perhaps nothing did more to impress the public mind—and this is true in all countries—than the assistance given in propaganda by intellectuals and literary notables. They were able to clothe the rough tissue of falsehood with phrases of literary merit and passages of eloquence better than the statesmen. Sometimes by expressions of spurious impartiality, at other times by rhetorical indignation, they could by their literary skill give this or that lie the stamp of indubitable authenticity, even without the shadow of a proof, or incidentally refer to it as an accepted fact. The narrowest patriotism could be made to appear noble, the foulest accusations could be represented as an indignant outburst of humanitarianism, and the meanest and most vindictive aims falsely disguised as idealism. Everything was legitimate which could make the soldiers go on fighting.

The frantic activity of ecclesiastics in recruiting by means of war propaganda made so deep an impression on the public mind that little comment on it is needed here. The few who courageously stood out became marked men. The resultant and significant loss of spiritual influence by the Churches is, in itself, sufficient evidence of the reaction against the betrayal in time of stress of the most elementary precepts of Christianity by those specially entrusted with the moral welfare of the people.

War is fought in this fog of falsehood, a great deal of

it undiscovered and accepted as truth. The fog arises from fear and is fed by panic. Any attempt to doubt or deny even the most fantastic story has to be condemned at once as unpatriotic, if not traitorous. This allows a free field for the rapid spread of lies. If they were only used to deceive the enemy in the game of war it would not be worth troubling about. But, as the purpose of most of them is to fan indignation and induce the flower of the country's youth to be ready to make the supreme sacrifice, it becomes a serious matter. Exposure, therefore, may be useful, even when the struggle is over, in order to show up the fraud, hypocrisy, and humbug on which all war rests, and the blatant and vulgar devices which have been used for so long to prevent the poor ignorant people from realizing the true meaning of war.

It must be admitted that many people were conscious and willing dupes. But many more were unconscious and were sincere in their patriotic zeal. Finding now that elaborately and carefully staged deceptions were practised on them, they feel a resentment which has not only served to open their eyes but may induce them to make their children keep their eyes open when next the bugle sounds.

Let us attempt a very faint and inadequate analogy between the conduct of nations and the conduct of individuals.

Imagine two large country houses containing large families with friends and relations. When the members of the family of the one house stay in the other, the butler is instructed to open all the letters they receive and send and inform the host of their contents, to listen at the keyhole, and tap the telephone. When a great match, say a cricket match, which excites the whole district, is played between them, those who are not present are given false reports of the game to make them think the side they favour is winning, the other side is accused of cheating and foul play, and scandalous reports are circulated about the head of the family and the hideous goings on in the other house.

All this, of course, is very mild, and there would be no specially dire consequences if people were to behave in such an inconceivably caddish, low, and underhand way, except that they would at once be expelled from decent society.

But between nations, where the consequences are vital, where the destiny of countries and provinces hangs in the balance, the lives and fortunes of millions are affected and civilization itself is menaced, the most upright men honestly believe that there is no depth of duplicity to which they may not legitimately stoop. They have got to do it. The thing cannot go on without the help of lies.

This is no plea that lies should not be used in war-time, but a demonstration of how lies *must* be used in war-time. If the truth were told from the outset, there would be no reason and no will for war.

Anyone declaring the truth: "Whether you are right or wrong, whether you win or lose, in no circumstances can war help you or your country," would find himself in gaol very quickly. In war-time, failure to lie is negligence, the doubting of a lie a misdemeanour, the declaration of the truth a crime.

In future wars we have now to look forward to a new and far more efficient instrument of propaganda—the Government control of broadcasting. Whereas, therefore, in the past we have used the word "broadcast" symbolically as meaning the efforts of the Press and individual reporters, in future we must use the word literally, since falsehood can now be circulated universally, scientifically, and authoritatively.

Many of the samples given in the assortment are international, but some are exclusively British, as these are more easily found and investigated, and, after all, we are more concerned with our own Government and Press methods and our own national honour than with the duplicity of other Governments.

Lies told in other countries are also dealt with in cases where it has been possible to collect sufficient data. Without special investigation on the spot, the career of particular lies cannot be fully set out.

When the people of one country understand how the people in another country are duped, like themselves, in war-time, they will be more disposed to sympathize with them as victims than condemn them as criminals, because they will understand that their crime only consisted in obedience to the dictates of authority and acceptance of what their Government and Press represented to them as the truth.

The period covered is roughly the four years of the war. The intensity of the lying was mitigated after 1918, although fresh crops came up in connection with other of our international relations. The mischief done by the false cry " Make Germany pay " continued after 1918 and led, more especially in France, to high expectations and consequent indignation when it was found that the people who raised this slogan knew all the time it was a fantastic impossibility. Many of the old war lies survived for several years, and some survive even to this day.

There is nothing sensational in the way of revelations contained in these pages. All the cases mentioned are well known to those who were in authority, less well known to those primarily affected, and unknown, unfortunately, to the millions who fell. Although only a small part of the vast field of falsehood is covered, it may suffice to show how the unsuspecting innocence of the masses in all countries was ruthlessly and systematically exploited.

There are some who object to war because of its immorality, there are some who shrink from the arbitrament of arms because of its increased cruelty and barbarity; there are a growing number who protest against this method, at the outset known to be unsuccessful, of attempting to settle international disputes because of its imbecility and futility. But there is not a living soul in any country who does not deeply resent having his passions roused, his indignation inflamed, his patriotism exploited, and his highest ideals desecrated by concealment, subterfuge, fraud, falsehood, trickery, and deliberate lying on the part of those in whom he is taught to repose confidence and to whom he is enjoined to pay respect.

None of the heroes prepared for suffering and sacrifice, none of the common herd ready for service and obedience, will be inclined to listen to the call of their country once they discover the polluted sources from whence that call proceeds and recognize the monstrous finger of falsehood which beckons them to the battlefield.

I

THE COMMITMENT TO FRANCE

OUR prompt entry into the European War in 1914 was necessitated by our commitment to France. This commitment was not known to the people; it was not known to Parliament; it was not even known to all the members of the Cabinet. More than this, its existence was denied. How binding the moral engagement was soon became clear. The fact that it was not a signed treaty had nothing whatever to do with the binding nature of an understanding come to as a result of military and naval conversations conducted over a number of years. Not only was it referred to as an " obligation of honour " (Lord Lansdowne), " A compact " (Mr. Lloyd George), " An honourable expectation " (Sir Eyre Crowe), " the closest negotiations and arrangements between the two Governments " (Mr. Austen Chamberlain), but Lord Grey himself has admitted that had we not gone in on France's side (quite apart from the infringement of Belgian neutrality), he would have resigned. That he should have pretended that we were not " bound " has been a matter of amazement to his warmest admirers, that the understanding should have been kept secret has been a subject of sharp criticism from statesmen of all parties. No more vital point stands out in the whole of pre-war diplomacy, and the bare recital of the denials, evasions, and subterfuges forms a tragic illustration of the low standard of national honour, where war is concerned, which is accepted by statesmen whose personal honour is beyond reproach.

It will be remembered that the conversations which involved close consultations between military and naval staffs began before 1906. The first explicit denial came in 1911. The subsequent extracts can be given with little further comment.

MR. JOWETT asked the Secretary of State for Foreign Affairs if, during his term of office, any undertaking, promise, or understanding had been given to France that, in certain eventualities, British troops would be sent to assist the operations of the French Army.

MR. McKINNON WOOD (Under-Secretary for Foreign Affairs): The answer is in the negative.

House of Commons, March 8, 1911.

SIR E. GREY: First of all let me try to put an end to some of the suspicions with regard to secrecy—suspicions with which it seems to me some people are torturing themselves, and certainly worrying others. We have laid before the House the Secret Articles of the Agreement with France of 1904. There are no other secret engagements. The late Government made that agreement in 1904. They kept those articles secret, and I think to everybody the reason will be obvious why they did so. It would have been invidious to make those articles public. In my opinion they were entirely justified in keeping those articles secret because they were not articles which commit this House to serious obligations. I saw a comment made the other day, when these articles were published, that if a Government would keep little things secret, *a fortiori*, they would keep big things secret. That is absolutely untrue. There may be reasons why a Government should make secret arrangements of that kind if they are not things of first-rate importance, if they are subsidiary to matters of great importance. But that is the very reason why the British Government should not make secret engagements which commit Parliament to obligations of war. It would be foolish to do it. No British Government could embark upon a war without public opinion behind it, and such engagements as there are which really commit Parliament to anything of the kind are contained in treaties or agreements which have been laid before the House. For ourselves, we have not made a single secret article of any kind since we came into office.

House of Commons, November 27, 1911.

The whole of this is a careful and deliberate evasion of the real point.

Nothing was clearer to everyone in Great Britain in August 1914 than that our understanding with France was a " secret engagement which committed Parliament to obligations of war."

Mr. Winston Churchill, in a memorandum to Sir E. Grey and the Prime Minister, August 23, 1912, wrote : " Everyone must feel who knows the facts that we have the obligations of an alliance without its advantages and, above all, without its precise definitions " (*The World Crisis*, vol. i, p. 115).

In 1912 M. Sazonov, the Russian Foreign Minister, reported to the Czar :

England promised to support France on land by sending an expedition of 100,000 to the Belgian border to repel the invasion of France by the German Army through Belgium, expected by the French General Staff.

LORD HUGH CECIL : . . . There is a very general belief that this country is under an obligation, not a treaty obligation, but an obligation arising owing to an assurance given by the Ministry in the course of diplomatic negotiations, to send a very large force out of this country to operate in Europe.

MR. ASQUITH : I ought to say that it is not true.

House of Commons, March 10, 1913.

SIR WILLIAM BYLES asked the Prime Minister whether

C

he will say if this country is under any, and if so, what, obligation to France to send an armed force in certain contingencies to operate in Europe; and if so, what are the limits of our agreements, whether by assurance or Treaty with the French nation.

MR. KING asked the Prime Minister (1) whether the foreign policy of this country is at the present time unhampered by any treaties, agreements, or obligations under which British military forces would, in certain eventualities, be called upon to be landed on the Continent and join there in military operations; and (2) whether in 1905, 1908, or 1911 this country spontaneously offered to France the assistance of a British army to be landed on the Continent to support France in the event of European hostilities.

MR. ASQUITH : As has been repeatedly stated, this country is not under any obligation not public and known to Parliament which compels it to take part in any war. In other words, if war arises between European Powers, there are no unpublished agreements which will restrict or hamper the freedom of the Government or of Parliament to decide whether or not Great Britain should participate in a war. The use that would be made of the naval and military forces if the Government or Parliament decided to take part in a war is, for obvious reasons, not a matter about which public statements can be made beforehand.

House of Commons, March 24, 1913.

SIR EDWARD GREY : I have assured the House, and the Prime Minister has assured the House more than once, that if any crisis such as this arose we should come before the House of Commons and be able to say to the House that it was free to decide what the attitude of the House should be; that we have no secret engagement which we should spring upon the House and tell the House that because we had entered upon that engagement there was an obligation of honour on the country. . . . I think [the letter] makes it perfectly clear that what the Prime Minister and I have said in the House of Commons was perfectly justified as regards our freedom to decide in a crisis what our line should be, whether we should intervene or whether we should abstain.

The Government remained perfectly free and *a fortiori* the House of Commons remained perfectly free.

House of Commons, August 3, 1914.

Yet all preparations to the last detail had been made, as shown by the prompt, secret, and well-organized dispatch of the Expeditionary Force.

As far back as January 31, 1906, Sir Edward Grey had written to our Ambassador at Paris describing a conversation with M. Cambon.

In the first place, since the Ambassador had spoken to me, a good deal of progress had been made. Our military and naval authorities had been in communication with the French, and I assumed that all preparations were ready, so that, if a crisis arose, no time would have been lost for want of a formal engagement.

Lord Grey writes in his book, *Twenty-Five Years* (published in 1925), with regard to his declaration in August 1914:

It will appear, if the reader looks back to the conversations with Cambon in 1906, that not only British and French military, but also naval, authorities were in consultation. But naval consultations had been put on a footing satisfactory to France in 1905, before the Liberal Government had come into office. The new step taken by us in January 1906 had been to authorize military conversations on the same footing as the naval ones. It was felt to be essential to make clear to the House that its liberty of decision was not hampered by any engagements entered into previously without its knowledge. Whatever obligation there was to France arose from what those must feel who had welcomed, approved, and sustained the Anglo-French friendship, that was open and known to all. In this connection there was nothing to disclose, except the engagement about the north and west coasts of France taken a few hours before, and the letters exchanged with Cambon in 1912, the letter that expressly stipulated there was no engagement.

One of the things which contributed materially to the unanimity of the country (on the outbreak of war) was that the Cabinet were able to come before Parliament and say that they had not made a secret agreement behind their backs.

Viscount Grey, receiving the Freedom of Glasgow, January 4, 1921. Reported in " The Times."

His constant repetition of this assurance is the best proof of his natural and obvious doubt that it was true.

But he continues the attempt at self-exculpation years after in his book, *Twenty-Five Years*. Outlining the considerations in his mind prior to the outbreak of war :

(3) That, if war came, the interest of Britain required that we should not stand aside while France fought alone in the west, but must support her. I knew it to be very doubtful whether the Cabinet, Parliament, and the country would take this view on the outbreak of war, and through the whole of this week I had in view the probable contingency that we should not decide at the critical moment to support France. In that event I should have to resign. . . .

(4) A clear view that no pledge must be given, no hope even held out to France and Russia which it was doubtful whether this country would fulfil. One danger I saw. . . . It was that France and Russia might face the ordeal of war with Germany relying on our support ; that this support might not be forthcoming, and that we might then, when it was too late, be held responsible by them for having let them in for a disastrous war. Of course I could resign if I gave them hopes which it turned out that the Cabinet and Parliament would not sanction. But what good would my resignation be to them in their ordeal ?

After quoting the King-Byles questions, June 11, 1914, he says :

The answer given is absolutely true. The criticism to which it is open is that it does not answer the question put to me. That is undeniable. Parliament has unqualified right to know of any agreements or arrangements that bind the country to action or restrain its freedom. But it cannot be told of military and naval measures to meet possible contingencies. So long as Governments are compelled to contemplate the possibility of war, they are under a necessity to take precautionary measures, the object of which would be defeated if they were made public. . . . If the question had been pressed, I must have declined to answer it and have given these reasons for doing so. Questions in the previous year about military arrangements with France had been put aside by the Prime Minister with a similar answer.

Neither the Franco-British military nor the Anglo-Russian naval conversations compromised the freedom of this country, but the latter were less intimate and important than the former. I was therefore quite justified in saying that the assurances given by the Prime Minister still held good. Nothing had been done that in any way weakened them, and this was the assurance that Parliament was entitled to have. Political engagements ought not to be kept secret; naval or military preparations for contingencies of war are necessary, but must be kept secret. In these instances care had been taken to ensure that such preparations did not involve any political engagement.

In the recently published official papers Sir Eyre Crowe, in a memorandum to Sir Edward Grey, July 31, 1914, says:

The argument that there is no written bond binding us to France is strictly correct. There is no contractual obligation. But the *Entente* has been made, strengthened, put to the test, and celebrated in a manner justifying the belief that a moral bond was being forged. The whole of the *Entente* can have no meaning if it does not signify that in a just quarrel England would stand by her friends. This honourable expectation has been raised. We cannot repudiate it without exposing our good name to grave criticism.

I venture to think that the contention that England cannot in any circumstances go to war is not true, and that any endorsement of it would be political suicide.

This is the plain common-sense official view which Sir E. Grey had before him. To insist that Parliament was free because the " honourable expectation " was not in writing was a deplorable subterfuge.

Lord Lansdowne, in the House of Lords on August 6, 1914, after referring to " Treaty obligations and those other obligations which are not less sacred because they are not embodied in signed and sealed documents," said :

Under the one category fall our Treaty obligations to Belgium. . . . To the other category belong our obligations to France—obligations of honour which have grown up in consequence of the close intimacy by which the two nations have been united during the last few years.

The idea that Parliament was free and was consulted on August 3rd also falls to the ground as a sham, owing to the fact that on August 2nd the naval protection of the French coast and shipping had been guaranteed by the Government. Parliament was not free in any case, owing to the commitments, but this made " consulta-tion " and parliamentary sanction an absolute farce.

As The Times said on August 5th, by this guarantee Great Britain was " definitely committed to the side of France " ; and M. Cambon, the French Ambassador, in an interview with M. Recouly, said : " A great country cannot make war half-way. The moment it has decided to fight on the sea it has fatally obligated itself to fight also on land." [1]

A Press opinion of the commitment may be given :

Take yet another instance which is fresh in everyone's recollection, viz. the arrangements as to the co-operation of the military staffs of Great Britain and France before the

---

[1] Les Heures tragiques d'avant Guerre, p. 55.

war. It was not until the very eve of hostilities that the House of Commons learned anything as to the nature of those arrangements. It was then explained by Sir Edward Grey that Great Britain was not definitely committed to go to the military assistance of France. There was no treaty. There was no convention. Great Britain, therefore, was free to give help or to withhold it, and yet, though there had been no formal commitment, we were fast bound by every consideration of honour, and the national conscience felt this instinctively, though it was only the invasion of Belgium which brought in the waverers and doubters. That situation arose out of secret diplomacy, and it is one which must never be allowed to spring again from the same cause. For we can conceive nothing more dangerous than for a Government to commit itself in honour, though not in technical fact, and then to make no adequate military preparations on the ground that the technical commitment has not been entered into.

" Daily Telegraph," September 1917.

Lord Haldane frankly admits, in *Before the War,* what he was doing in 1906. He says that the problem which presented itself to him in 1906 was "how to mobilize and concentrate at a place of assembly to be opposite the Belgian frontier," a British expeditionary force of 160,000.

MR. LLOYD GEORGE (speaking of the beginning of the war): We had a compact with France that if she were wantonly attacked, the United Kingdom would go to her support.

MR. HOGGE: We did not know that!

MR. LLOYD GEORGE: If France were wantonly attacked.

AN HON. MEMBER: That is news.

MR. LLOYD GEORGE: There was no compact as to what force we should bring into the arena. . . . Whatever arrangements we come to, I think history will show that we have more than kept faith.

House of Commons, August 7, 1918.

In spite, then, of Lord Grey's assurances of the freedom of Parliament, it becomes clear that had Parliament taken the other course, Great Britain would have broken faith with France.

Some foreign opinions may be given :

In the French Chamber, September 3, 1919, M. Franklin-Bouillon, criticizing the Triple Alliance, suggested in 1919 between French, British, and American Governments, declared that France was better protected by the Anglo-French understanding of 1912, " which assured us the support of six divisions," and—upon an interruption by M. Tardieu—agreed that the " text " of the understanding did not specify six divisions, but that staff collaboration had " prearranged everything for the mobilization and immediate embarkation of six divisions."

In April 1913 M. Sazonov reported to the Czar :

Without hesitating, Grey stated that should the conditions under discussion arise, England would stake everything in order to inflict the most serious blow to German power. . . . Arising out of this, Grey, upon his own initiative, corroborated what I already knew from Poincaré, the existence of an agreement between France and Great Britain, according to which England engaged itself, in case of a war with Germany, not only to come to the assistance of France on the sea, but also on the Continent by landing troops.

The intervention of England in the war had been anticipated.   A military convention existed with England which could not be divulged as it bore a secret character.   We relied upon six English divisions and upon the assistance of the Belgians.
Marshall Joffre before a Paris Commission, July 5, 1919.

A comparison of the successive plans of campaign of the French General Staff enables us to determine the exact moment when English co-operation, in consequence of these promises, became part of our military strategy. Plan 16 did not allow for it ; Plan 16A, drawn up in September 1911, takes into account the presence of an English Army on our left wing. The Minister of War (Messimy) said: "Our conversations with General Wilson, representing the British General Staff at the time of the Agadir affair, enabled us to have the certainty of English intervention in the event of a conflict." The representative of the British General Staff had promise of the help of 100,000 men, but stipulating that they should land in France because, as he argued, a landing at Antwerp would take much longer.

From " La Victoire," by Fabre Luce.

The British and French General Staffs had for years been in close consultation with one another on this subject. The area of concentration for the British forces had been fixed on the left flank of the French and the actual detraining stations of the various units were all laid down in terrain lying between Maubeuge and Le Cateau. The headquarters of the army were fixed at the latter place.

Lord French's book on the war, 1919.

As to the danger of the secrecy which was the cause of the denials and evasions, three quotations may be given.

MR. BONAR LAW: . . . It has been said—and I think it is very likely true—that if Germany had known for certain that Great Britain would have taken part in the war, the war would never have occurred.

House of Commons, July 18, 1918.

Lord Loreburn, in *How the War Came*, says: "The concealment from the Cabinet was protracted and must have been deliberate."

MR. AUSTEN CHAMBERLAIN : . . . We found ourselves on a certain Monday listening to a speech by Lord Grey at this box which brought us face to face with war and upon which followed our declaration. That was the first public notification to the country, or to anyone by the Government of the day, of the position of the British Government and of the obligations which it had assumed. . . . Was the House of Commons free to decide? Relying upon the arrangements made between the two Governments, the French coast was undefended—I am not speaking of Belgium, but of France. There had been the closest negotiations and arrangements between our two Governments and our two staffs. There was not a word on paper binding this country, but in honour it was bound as it had never been bound before—I do not say wrongfully; I think rightly.

MR. T. P. O'CONNOR: It should not have been secret.

MR. CHAMBERLAIN: I agree. That is my whole point, and I am coming to it. Can we ever be indifferent to the French frontier or to the fortunes of France? A friendly Power in possession of the Channel ports is a British interest, treaty or no treaty. . . . Suppose that engagement had been made publicly in the light of day. Suppose it had been laid before this House and approved by this House, might not the events of those August days have been different? . . . If we had had that, if our obligations had been known and definite, it is at least possible, and I think it is probable, that war would have been avoided in 1914.

House of Commons, February 8, 1922.

There can be no question, therefore, that the deliberate denials and subterfuges, kept up till the last moment and fraught as they were with consequences of such magnitude, constitute a page in the history of secret diplomacy which is without parallel and afford a signal illustration of the slippery slope of official concealments.

II

SERBIA AND THE MURDER OF THE ARCHDUKE

THE murder at Serajevo of the Archduke `Franz Ferdinand, nephew of the Emperor Francis Joseph, and the consequent Austrian ultimatum, are sometimes referred to as the cause of the war, whereas, of course, they were only the occasion—the match which set fire to the well-stored powder magazine. The incident was by no means a good one for propaganda purposes. Fortunately for the Government, the Serajevo assassination, together with the secret commitment to France, was allowed to fall into the background after the invasion of Belgium. It was extremely difficult to make the Serbian cause popular. *John Bull* exploded at once with " To Hell with Serbia," and most people were naturally averse to being dragged into a European war for such a cause. Some wondered what the attitude of our own Government would have been had the Prince of Wales been murdered in similar circumstances, and a doubtful frame of mind existed. The Serbian case, therefore, had to be written up, and " poor little Serbia " had to be presented as an innocent small nationality subjected to the offensive brutality of the Austrians.

The following extract from *The Times* leader, September 15, 1914, is a good sample of how public opinion was worked up :

The letter which we publish this morning from Sir Valentine Chirol is a welcome reminder of the duty we owe

to the gallant army and people. . . . We are too apt to
overlook the splendid heroism of the Servian people and
the sacrifices they have incurred. . . . And Servia has
amply deserved support. . . . Nor ought we to forget that
this European war of liberation was precipitated by Austro-
German aggression upon Servia. The accusations of
complicity in the Sarajevo crime launched against Servia as
a pretext for aggression have not been proved. It is more
than doubtful whether they are susceptible of proof. . . .
While there is thus every reason for not accepting Austrian
charges, there are the strongest reasons for giving effective
help to a gallant ally who has fought for a century in defence
of the principle of the independence of little States which
we ourselves are now fighting to vindicate with all the
resources of our Empire.

Mr. Lloyd George, speaking at the Queen's Hall on
September 21, 1914, said:

If any Servians were mixed up with the murder of the
Archduke, they ought to be punished for it. Servia admits
that. The Servian Government had nothing to do with it.
Not even Austria claimed that. The Servian Prime Minister
is one of the most capable and honoured men in Europe.
Servia was willing to punish any of her subjects who had
been proved to have any complicity in that assassination.
What more could you expect?

Punch gave us "Heroic Serbia," a gallant Serb
defending himself on a mountain pass.

Between June 28 and July 23, 1914, no arrests were
made or explanation given by the Serbian Government.
The Austrian representative, Von Storck, was told:
" The police have not concerned themselves with the
affair." The impression given was that entirely irre-
sponsible individuals, unknown to anyone in authority,
were the criminals. As the war proceeded the matter
was lost sight of, and our Serbian ally and its Govern-

ment were universally accepted as one of the small outraged nationalities for whose liberation and rights British soldiers were willingly prepared to sacrifice their lives.

The revelations as to the complicity of the Serbian Government in the crime did not appear till 1924, when an article was published entitled, " After Vidovdan, 1914," by Ljuba Jovanovitch, President of the Serbian Parliament, who had been Minister of Education in the Cabinet of M. Pashitch in 1914. The relevant extracts fron this article may be given.

I do not remember if it were the end of May or the beginning of June when, one day, M. Pashitch told us that certain persons were preparing to go to Serajevo, in order to kill Franz Ferdinand, who was expected there on Vidovdan (Sunday, June 28th). He told this much to us others, but he acted further in the affair only with Stojan Protitch, then Minister of the Interior. As they told me afterwards, this was prepared by a society of secretly organized men, and by the societies of patriotic students of Bosnia-Herzegovina, in Belgrade. M. Pashitch and we others said (and Stojan Protitch agreed) that he, Stojan, should order the authorities on the Drin frontier to prevent the crossing of the youths who had left Belgrade for the purpose. But these frontier authorities were themselves members of the organization, and did not execute Stojan's order, and told him, and he afterwards told us, that the order had come too late, for the youths had already crossed over. Thus failed the Government attempt to prevent the outrage (*atentat*) that had been prepared.

This makes it clear that the whole Cabinet knew of the plot some time before the murder took place ; that the Prime Minister and Minister of the Interior knew in which societies it had been prepared ; that the frontier guard was deeply implicated and working under the orders of those who were arranging the crime.

There failed also the attempt of our Minister of Vienna, made on his own initiative, to the Minister Bilinski, to turn the Archduke from the fatal path which had been planned. Thus the death of the Archduke was accomplished in circumstances more awful than had been foreseen and with consequences no one could have even dreamed of.

No official instruction was sent to Vienna to warn the Archduke. The Minister acted on his own initiative. This is further substantiated by a statement of M. Pashitch quoted in the *Standard*, July 21, 1914.

Had we known of the plot against the late Archduke Franz Ferdinand, assuredly we should have informed the Austro-Hungarian Government.

He did know of the plot, but gave no warning to the Austro-Hungarian Government.

In an article in the *Neues Wiener Tageblatt*, June 28, 1924, Jovan Jovanovitch, the Serbian Minister in Vienna, explained that the warning he gave was in the form of a personal and unprompted opinion that the manœuvres were provocative and the Archduke might be shot by one of his own troops.

Ljuba Javanovitch describes his reception of the news :

On Vidovdan (Sunday, June 28, 1914) in the afternoon I was at my country house at Senjak. About 5 p.m. an official telephoned to me from the Press Bureau telling what had happened at Serajevo. And although I knew what was being prepared there, yet, as I held the receiver, it was as though someone had unexpectedly dealt me a heavy blow. When later the news was confirmed from other quarters a heavy anxiety oppressed me. . . . I saw that the position of our Government with regard to other Governments would be very difficult, far worse than after May 29, 1903 (the murder of King Alexander).

In *La Fédération Balcanique* Nicola Nenadovitch asserts that King Alexander, the Russian Minister Hartwig, and the Russian military attaché Artmanov, as well as Pashitch, were privy to the plot.

The Austrian Government, in its ultimatum, demanded the arrest of one Ciganovitch. He was found, but mysteriously disappeared. This man played an important part. Colonel Simitch, in *Clarté*, May 1925, describes him as a link between Pashitch and the conspirators, and says : " M. Pashitch sent his agent into Albania." The report of the Salonika trial shows that he was a spy and agent provocateur to the Serb Government. He was "Number 412" in the list of "the Black Hand," a revolutionary society known to and encouraged by the Government (M. Pashitch's nephew was a member). Its head was Dimitrijevitch, the chief officer of the Intelligence Staff, an outstanding figure who led the assassination of King Alexander and his Queen in 1903. The agent of the Black Hand in Serajevo was Gatchinovitch, who organized the murder, plans having been laid months beforehand. The first attempt with a bomb was made by Chabrinovitch, who was in the Serbian State printing office. Printzip, a wild young man who was simply a tool, actually committed the murder. When he and the other murderers were arrested they confessed that it was through Ciganovitch that they had been introduced to Major Tankositch, supplied with weapons and given shooting lessons. After the Salonika trial the Pashitch Government sent Ciganovitch, as a reward for his services, to America with a false passport under the name of Danilovitch. After the war was over Ciganovitch returned, and the Government gave him some land near Uskub, where he then resided.

That the Austrian Government should have recognized
that refusal to either find Ciganovitch or permit others
to look for him meant guilt on the part of the Serbian
Government and therefore resorted to war is not
surprising.

A postcard was found at Belgrade " poste restante,"
written from Serajevo by one of the criminals to one of
his comrades in Belgrade.   But this was not followed
up.   As Ljuba says :

On the whole it could be expected that Vienna would
not succeed in proving any connection between official
Serbia and the event on the Miljacka.

The remark of a Serbian student sums up the case :
" You see, the plan was quite successful.   We have
made Great Serbia."   And M. Pashitch himself, on
August 13, 1915, declared :

Never in history has there been a better outlook for the
Serbian nation than has arisen since the outbreak of war.

It came as a surprise to the Serbian Government that
any excitement should have been caused by the revelation
of Ljuba.   They thought that Great Britain understood
what had happened, and in her eagerness to fight
Germany had jumped at the excuse.   When, however,
the truth came out, proceedings were instituted to
expel Ljuba from the Radical Party.   Nothing which
transpired on this occasion, however, produced a
categorical denial from M. Pashitch of the charge made
by Ljuba.   He evaded the issue so far as possible.

There appears to be no doubt that before the end of
the war the British War Office was officially informed
that Dimitrijevitch, of the Serbian Intelligence Staff,
was the prime author of the murder.   He was executed

at Salonika in 1917, his existence having been found to be inconvenient. But when it came to the framing of the Peace Treaties at Versailles, there was a conspiracy of silence on the whole subject.

This terrible instance of deception should be classed as a Serbian lie, but its acceptance was so widespread that half Europe became guilty of complicity in it, and even if the truth did reach other Chancelleries and Foreign Offices of the Allied Powers during the war, it would have been quite impossible for them to reveal it. Had the truth been known, however, in July 1914, the opinion of the British people with regard to the Austrian ultimatum would have been very different from what it was.

III

INVASION OF BELGIUM AS CAUSE OF WAR

WHATEVER may have been the causes of the Great War, the German invasion of Belgium was certainly not one of them. It was one of the first consequences of war. Nor was it even the reason of our entry into the war. But the Government, realizing how doubtful it was whether they could rouse public enthusiasm over a secret obligation to France, was able, owing to Germany's fatal blunder, to represent the invasion of Belgium and the infringement of the Treaty of Neutrality as the cause of our participation in it.

We know now that we were committed to France by an obligation of honour, we know now that Sir Edward Grey would have resigned had we not gone in on the side of France, and we also know that Mr. Bonar Law committed the Conservative Party to the support of war *before* the question of the invasion of Belgium arose.

The Government already know, but I give them now the assurance on behalf of the party of which I am Leader in this House, that in whatever steps they think it necessary to take for the honour and security of this country, they can rely on the unhesitating support of the Opposition.

Quoted in " Twenty-Five Years," by Viscount Grey.

The invasion of Belgium came as a godsend to the Government and the Press, and they jumped to take advantage of this pretext, fully appreciating its value from the point of view of rallying public opinion.

We are going into a war that is forced upon us as the defenders of the weak and the champions of the liberties of Europe.

" The Times," August 5, 1914.

It should be clearly understood when it was and why it was we intervened. It was only when we were confronted with the choice between keeping and breaking solemn obligations, between the discharge of a binding trust and of shameless subservience to naked force, that we threw away the scabbard. . . . We were bound by our obligations, plain and paramount, to assert and maintain the threatened independence of a small and neutral State (Belgium).

Mr. Asquith, House of Commons, August 27, 1914.

The treaty obligations of Great Britain to that little land (Belgium) brought us into the war.

Mr. Lloyd George, January 5, 1918.

Neither of these statements by successive Prime Ministers is true. We were drawn into the war because of our commitment to France. The attack on Belgium was used to excite national enthusiasm. A phrase to the same effect was inserted in the King's Speech of September 18, 1914.

I was compelled in the assertion of treaty obligations deliberately set at naught . . . to go to war.

The two following extracts put the matter correctly :

They do not reflect that our honour and our interest must have compelled us to join France and Russia even if Germany had scrupulously respected the rights of her small neighbours, and had sought to hack her way into France through the Eastern fortresses.

" The Times," March 15, 1915.

Sir D. Maclean : We went into the war on account of Belgium.

Mr. Chamberlain : We had such a treaty with Belgium.

Had it been France only, we could not have stayed out
after the conversations that had taken place. It would not
have been in our interests to stay out, and we could not
have stayed out without loss of security and honour.
House of Commons, February 8, 1922.

But in addition to the attack on Belgium being
declared to be the cause of the war, it was also represented as an unprecedented and unwarrantable breach of
a treaty. To this day "the Scrap of Paper" (a
facsimile of the treaty) is framed on the walls of some
elementary schools.

There is no nation which has not been guilty of the
breach of a treaty. After war is declared, treaties are
scrapped right and left. There were other infringe-
ments of neutrality during the war. The infringement
of a treaty is unfortunately a matter of expediency, not
a matter of international morality. In 1887, when there
was a scare of an outbreak of war between France and
Germany, the Press, including the *Standard,* which
was regarded at that time more or less as a Government organ, discussed dispassionately and with calm
equanimity the possibility of allowing Germany to pass
through Belgium in order to attack France. The
Standard argued that it would be madness for Great
Britain to oppose the passage of German troops through
Belgium, and the *Spectator* said : "We shall not bar, as
indeed we cannot bar, the traversing of her soil." We
were not more sensitive to our treaty obligations in
1914 than we were in 1887. But it happened that in
1887 we were on good terms with Germany and on
strained terms with France. The opposite policy,
therefore, suited our book better.

Moreover, the attack on Belgium did not come as a
surprise. All our plans were made in preparation for it.

The Belgian documents which were published disclosed the fact that the "conversations" of 1906 concerned very full plans for military co-operation in the event of a German invasion of Belgium, but similar plans were not drawn up between Belgium and Germany. The French and British are referred to as the *Allied* armies, Germany as "the enemy." Full and elaborate plans were made for the landing of British troops.

Politically the invasion of Belgium was a gross error. Strategically it was the natural and obvious course to take. Further, we know now that had Germany not violated Belgian neutrality, France would have. The authority for this information, which from the point of view of military strategy is perfectly intelligible, is General Percin, whose articles in *l'Ère Nouvelle* in 1925 are thus quoted and commented on in the *Manchester Guardian* of January 27, 1925.

VIOLATION OF BELGIAN NEUTRALITY INTENDED BY FRANCE.

ALLEGATIONS BY A FRENCH GENERAL.

(From our own Correspondent.)

PARIS, *Monday.*

Immediately before Great Britain's entry into the war in 1914 the British Government inquired both in Berlin and Paris whether Belgian neutrality was going to be respected. Was the addressing of this inquiry to France a pure matter of form?

If General Percin, the well-known Radical non-Catholic French General, is to be believed, apparently not, for he declares authoritatively in a series of articles that he has begun in the *Ère Nouvelle* that the violation of Belgian neutrality had for many years been an integral part of the war plans of the French General Staff and even of the French Government.

The controversy that has started, it need hardly be said, is of world importance, for it disposes in a large moral degree of the Scrap of Paper stigma against Germany.

General Percin, it must be admitted, is an embittered man, though no one has yet been found to question his honour or capacity. He is a Protestant—a rare thing in the high ranks of the French Army—and has always been at loggerheads with the military hierarchy of the General Staff. That is little wonder, for he was chief of the Cabinet to General André, Minister of War in the Combes Cabinet, when in the Dreyfus affair a more or less vain effort was made to purge the High Command. General Percin's principal interest was in artillery, and the German papers during the war credited him with having been principally responsible for the adoption of the famous ·75. The deposition of General Percin from the military command at Lisle in the first few weeks of the war has never been clearly explained. It seems to have been part of a vendetta. At any rate, that no disgrace was implied was shown by the later grant to him of the Grand Cordon of the Legion of Honour.

A DISCOVERY OF 1910–11.

General Percin's evidence in *Ere Nouvelle* dates from the time when he was one of the chiefs of the Superior Council of War. " I took a personal part," he writes, " in the winter of 1910–11 in a great campaign organized in the Superior Council of War, of which I was then a member. The campaign lasted a week. It showed that a German attack on the Alsace-Lorraine front had no chance of success ; that it would inevitably be smashed against the barriers accumulated in that region, and that (Germany would) be obliged to violate Belgian neutrality.

" The question was not discussed whether we should follow the German lead in such violation and if necessary anticipate it ourselves, or whether we should await the enemy on this side of the Belgian frontier. That was a question of a Governmental rather than of a military kind. But any commander of troops who in time of war learns that the enemy has the intention of occupying a point the position of which gives him tactical advantage has the imperative duty to try to occupy that point first himself, and as soon as ever he can. If any of us had said that out of respect for the treaty of 1839 he would on his own initiative have remained on this side of the Belgian frontier, thus bringing the war on to French territory, he would have been scorned by his comrades and by the Minister of War himself.

"We were all of us in the French army partisans of the tactical offensive. It implied the violation of Belgian neutrality, for we knew the intentions of the Germans. I shall be told that on our part it would not have been a French crime, but a retort, a riposte to a German crime. No doubt. But every entry into war professes to be such a riposte. You attack the enemy because you attribute to him the intention of attacking you."

On August 31, 1911, the Chiefs of the French and Russian General Staffs signed an agreement that the words "defensive war" should not be taken literally, and then affirmed "the absolute necessity for the French and Russian armies of taking a vigorous offensive as far as possible simultaneously."

According to General Percin, that "vigorous offensive" meant French violation of Belgian neutrality.

"Could we take a vigorous offensive without the violation of Belgian neutrality? Could we really deploy our 1,300,000 men on the narrow front of Alsace-Lorraine?"

Violation of Belgium Inevitable.

He asserts categorically that in the mind of the French General Staff the war was to take place in Belgium, and, indeed, six months after the signature of the agreement between the French and Russian General Staffs quoted above, Artillery-Colonel Picard, at the head of a group of officers of the General Staff, made a tour in Belgium to study utilization, when the time should come, of this field of operations.

General Percin concludes : "The treaty of 1839 could not help but be violated either by the Germans or by us. It had been invented to make war impossible. The question that we have to judge upon, then, is this : Which of the two, France or Germany, wanted war the most ? Not which showed most contempt for this treaty. The one that willed war more than the other could not help but will the violation of Belgian territory."

A number of extracts might be given to show that the invasion of Belgium was expected. Yet no steps were taken in the years before the war to reaffirm the obligations under the old treaty of 1839 and make them a great deal more binding than in actual fact they were.

The invasion of Belgium was *not* the cause of the war; the invasion of Belgium was *not* unexpected; the invasion of Belgium did *not* shock the moral susceptibilities of either the British or French Governments. But it may be admitted that, finding themselves in the position which they had themselves largely contributed to create, the British and French Governments in the first stages of the Great War were fully justified, and indeed urgently compelled, to arrange the facts and distort the implications as they did, given always the standard of morality which war involves. To colour the picture with the pigment of falsehood so as to excite popular indignation was imperative, and it was done with complete success.

IV

GERMANY'S SOLE RESPONSIBILITY
FOR THE WAR

THE accusation against the enemy of *sole* responsibility for the war is common form in every nation and in every war. So far as we are concerned, the Russians (in the Crimean War), the Afghans, the Arabs, the Zulus, and the Boers, were each in their turn unprovoked aggressors, to take only some recent instances. It is a necessary falsehood based on a momentary biased opinion of one side in a dispute, and it becomes the indispensable basis of all subsequent propaganda. Leading articles in the newspapers at the outbreak of every war ring the changes on this theme, and are so similarly worded as to make it almost appear as if standard articles are set up in readiness and the name of the enemy, whoever he may be, inserted when the moment comes. Gradually the accusation is dropped officially, when reason returns and the consolidation of peace becomes an imperative necessity for all nations.

It is hardly necessary to give many instances of the universal declaration of Germany's sole responsibility, criminality, and evil intention. Similar declarations might be collected in each country on *both* sides in the war.

It [the declaration of war] is hardly surprising news, for a long chain of facts goes to show that Germany has deliberately brought on the crisis which now hangs over Europe.
                                                    "The Times," August 5, 1914.

Germany and Austria have alone wanted this war.
Sir Valentine Chirol, " The Times," August 6, 1914.

And with whom does this responsibility rest ? . . . One
Power, and one Power only, and that Power is Germany.
Mr. Asquith at the Guildhall, September 4, 1914.

(We are fighting) to defeat the most dangerous conspiracy ever plotted against the liberty of nations, carefully,
skilfully, insidiously, clandestinely planned in every detail
with ruthless, cynical determination.
Mr. Lloyd George, August 4, 1917.

Lord Northcliffe, who was in charge of war propaganda, saw how essential it was to make the accusation
the basis of all his activities. " The whole situation of
the Allies in regard to Germany is governed by the
fact that Germany is responsible for the war," and
again, " The Allies must never be tired of insisting that
they were the victims of a deliberate aggression "
(*Secrets of Crewe House*).

Among the few moderate voices in August 1914 was
Lord Rosebery, who wrote :

It was really a spark in the midst of the great powder
magazine which the nations of Europe have been building
up for the last twenty or thirty years. . . . I do not know
if there was some great organizer. . . . Without evidence I
should be loath to lay such a burthen on the head of any man.

So violently and repeatedly, however, had the accusa-
tion been made in all the Allied countries, that the
Government were forced to introduce it into the Peace
Treaty.

Article 231.—The Allied and Associated Governments
affirm and Germany accepts the responsibility of Germany
and her allies for causing all the loss and damage to which
the Allied and Associated Governments and their nationals

have been subjected as a consequence of the war imposed upon them by the aggression of Germany and her allies.

When war passions began to subside, the accusation was gradually dropped. The statesmen themselves even withdrew it.

The more one reads memoirs and books written in the various countries of what happened before August 1, 1914, the more one realizes that no one at the head of affairs quite meant war at that stage. It was something into which they glided, or rather staggered and stumbled, perhaps through folly, and a discussion, I have no doubt, would have averted it.

Mr. Lloyd George, December 23, 1920.

I cannot say that Germany and her allies were solely responsible for the war which devastated Europe. . . . That statement, which we all made during the war, was a weapon to be used at the time ; now that the war is over it cannot be used as a serious argument. . . . When it will be possible to examine carefully the diplomatic documents of the war, and time will allow us to judge them calmly, it will be seen that Russia's attitude was the real and underlying cause of the world conflict.

Signor Francesco Nitti, former Premier of Italy.

Is there any man or woman—let me say, is there any child—who does not know that the seed of war in the modern world is industrial and commercial rivalry ? . . . This was an industrial and commercial war.

President Woodrow Wilson, September 5, 1919.

I do not claim that Austria or Germany in the first place had a conscious thought-out intention of provoking a general war. No existing documents give us the right to suppose that at that time they had planned anything so systematic.

M. Raymond Poincaré, 1925.

I dare say that the belief in the sole guilt of Germany is not possible even to M. Poincaré. But if one can construct a policy based upon the theory of Germany's sole guilt, it is clear that one should grimly stick to this theory, or at least give oneself the appearance of conviction.

> *General Sukhomlinoff (Russian Minister of War). Quoted by M. Vaillant Conturier in the Chamber of Deputies (" Journal Officiel," July 5, 1922).*

The Press and publicists also changed their tone.

To saddle Germany with the sole responsibility for the war is from what we already know—and more will come—an absurdity. To frame a treaty on an absurdity is an injustice. Humanly, morally, and historically the Treaty of Versailles stands condemned, quite apart from its economic monstrosities.

> *Austin Harrison, Editor " English Review."*

Did vindictive nations ever do anything meaner, falser, or more cruel than when the Allies, by means of the Versailles Treaty, forced Germany to be the scapegoat to bear the guilt which belonged to all? What nation carries clean hands and a pure heart?

> *Charles F. Dole.*

In 1923 the representatives of the nations assembled on a Temporary Mixed Commission to draft a Treaty of Mutual Assistance under the auspices of the League of Nations. Fully aware of what had been declared to be by their Governments a flagrant and indisputable instance of unprovoked aggression on the part of Germany, they found themselves quite unable to define " unprovoked aggression." The Belgian, Brazilian, French, and Swedish delegations said, in the course of a memorandum :

It is not enough merely to repeat the formula " unprovoked aggression," for under the conditions of modern warfare it would seem impossible to decide even in theory what constitutes a case of aggression.

This view was practically adopted and the Committee of Jurists, when consulted, suggested that the term "aggression" should be dropped. The future case under the Covenant of the League of Nations of a nation which refused the recommendation of the Council or the verdict of the Court and resorted to arms was substituted as constituting a war of aggression.

In 1925, in the preamble of the Locarno Pact drawn up between Germany, France, and Great Britain, there is not the faintest echo of the accusation ; on the contrary, a phrase is actually inserted as follows :

Anxious to satisfy the desire for security and protection which animates the peoples upon whom fell the scourge of the war 1914–1918 (les nations qui ont en à subir le fléau de la guerre).

This is no place to enter into the question of responsibility, to shift the blame from one nation to another, or to show the degree in which Germany was indeed responsible.   Sole responsibility is a very different thing from some responsibility.   The Germans and Austrians were busy, not without good evidence, in accusing Russia.   But the disputes and entanglements and the deplorable ineptitude of diplomacy on all sides in the last few weeks were not, any more than the murder of the Archduke, the cause of the war, although special documents are always produced to give the false impression.

The causes were precedent and far-reaching, and it is doubtful if even the historians of the future will be able to apportion the blame between the Powers concerned with any degree of accuracy.

Lord Cecil of Chelwood recently put his finger on the most undoubted of all the contributory and immediate causes. Speaking in the City in 1927, he referred to " the gigantic competition in armaments before the war," and said :

No one could deny that the state of mind produced by armament competitions prepared the soil on which grew up the terrible plant which ultimately fruited in the Great War.

The above series of quotations will suffice to show how the sole culpability of the enemy is, as always, a war-time myth. The great success of the propaganda, however, leaves the impression fixed for a long time on the minds of those who want to justify to themselves their action in supporting the war and of those who have not taken the trouble to follow the subsequent withdrawals and denials. Moreover, the myth is allowed to remain, so far as possible, in the public mind in the shape of fear of " unprovoked aggression," and becomes the chief, and indeed the sole, justification for preparations for another war.

V

PASSAGE OF RUSSIAN TROOPS THROUGH GREAT BRITAIN

No obsession was more widespread through the war than the belief in the last months of 1914 that Russian troops were passing through Great Britain to the Western Front. Nothing illustrates better the credulity of the public mind in war-time and what favourable soil it becomes for the cultivation of falsehood.

How the rumour actually originated it is difficult to say. There were subsequently several more or less humorous suggestions made : of a telegram announcing the arrival of a large number of Russian eggs, referred to as " Russians " ; of the tall, bearded individual who declared from the window of a train that he came from " Ross-shire " ; and of the excited French officer with imperfect English pronunciation who went about near the front, exclaiming, " Where are de rations." But General Sukhomlinoff, in his memoirs, states that Sir George Buchanan, the British Ambassador in Russia, actually requested the dispatch of " a complete Russian army corps " to England, and English ships were to be brought to Archangel for the transport of these troops. The Russian General Staff, he adds, came to the conclusion that " Buchanan had lost his reason."

Whatever the origin may have been, the rumour spread like wild-fire, and testimony came from every part of the country from people who had seen the

Russians. They were in trains with the blinds down, on platforms stamping the snow off their boots; they called hoarsely for "vodka" at Carlisle and Berwick-on-Tweed, and they jammed the penny-in-the-slot machine with a rouble at Durham. The number of troops varied according to the imaginative powers of the witness.

As the rumour had undoubted military value, the authorities took no steps to deny it. A telegram from Rome appeared giving "the official news of the concentration of 250,000 Russian troops in France." With regard to this telegram the official Press Bureau stated: "That there was no confirmation of the statements contained in it, but that there was no objection to them being published." As there was a strict censorship of news, the release of this telegram served to confirm the rumour and kept the false witnesses busy.

On September 9, 1914, the following appeared in the *Daily News*:

The official sanction to the publication of the above (the telegram from Rome) removes the newspaper reserve with regard to the rumours which for the last fortnight have coursed with such astonishing persistency through the length and breadth of England. Whatever be the unvarnished truth about the Russian forces in the West, so extraordinary has been the ubiquity of the rumours in question, that they are almost more amazing if they are false than if they are true. Either a baseless rumour has obtained a currency and a credence perhaps unprecedented in history, or, incredible as it may appear, it is a fact that Russian troops, whatever the number may be, have been disembarked and passed through this country, while not one man in ten thousand was able to say with certainty whether their very existence was not a myth.

The Press on the whole, was reserved, fearing a

trap, and the *Daily Mail* suggested that the Russian Consul-General's statement that " about 5,000 Russian reservists have permission to serve the Allies " might be at the bottom of the rumour.   Like a popular book, the rumour spread more from verbal personal communications than on account of Press notices.

On September 14, 1914, the *Daily News* again returned to the subject :

As will be seen from the long dispatch of Mr. P. J. Philip, our special correspondent, Russian troops are now co-operating with the Belgians.   This information proves the correctness of the general impression that Russian troops have been moved through England.

"Daily News," September 14, 1914.

(*Dispatch.*)

To-night, in an evening paper, I find the statement " de bonne source " that the German Army in Belgium has been cut . . . by the Belgian *Army reinforced by Russian* troops. The last phrase unseals my pen.   For two days I have been on a long trek looking for the Russians, and now I have found them—where and how it would not be discreet to tell, but the published statement that they are here is sufficient, and of my own knowledge I can answer for their presence.

An official War Office denial of the rumour was noted by the *Daily News* on September 16, 1914.

The *Daily Mail*, September 9, 1914, contained a facetious article on the Russian rumour, concluding :

But now we are told from Rome that the Russians are in France.   How are we all going to apologize to the Bernets, Brocklers, and Pendles—if they were right, after all ?

Mr. King asked the Under-Secretary of State for War whether he can state, without injury to the military interests

E

of the Allies, whether any Russian troops have been conveyed through Great Britain to the Western area of the European War?

THE UNDER-SECRETARY OF STATE FOR WAR (Mr. Tennant): I am uncertain whether it will gratify or displease my hon. friend to learn that no Russian troops have been conveyed through Great Britain to the Western area of the European War.

House of Commons, November 18, 1914

VI

THE MUTILATED NURSE

MANY atrocity stories were circulated which were impossible to prove or disprove, but in the early months of the war the public was shocked by a horrible story of barbarous cruelty, of which a complete record can be given. It is a curious instance of the ingenuity of the deliberate individual liar.

A NURSE'S TRAGEDY.

DUMFRIES GIRL THE VICTIM OF SHOCKING BARBARITY.

News has reached Dumfries of the shocking death of a Dumfries young woman, Nurse Grace Hume, who went out to Belgium at the outbreak of war. Nurse Hume was engaged at the camp hospital at Vilvorde, and she was the victim of horrible cruelty at the hands of German soldiers. Her breasts were cut off and she died in great agony. Nurse Hume's family received a note written shortly before she died. It was dated September 6th, and ran: "Dear Kate, this is to say good-bye. Have not long to live. Hospital has been set on fire. Germans cruel. A man here had his head cut off. My right breast has been taken away. Give my love to —— Good-bye. GRACE."

Nurse Hume's left breast was cut away after she had written the note. She was a young woman of twenty-three and was formerly a nurse in Huddersfield Hospital.

Nurse Mullard, of Inverness, delivered the note personally to Nurse Hume's sister at Dumfries. She was also at Vilvorde, and she states that Nurse Hume acted the part of a heroine. A German attacked a wounded soldier whom

Nurse Hume was taking to hospital. The nurse took his gun and shot the German dead.

"*The Star*," *September* 16, 1914.

LETTER DELIVERED BY NURSE MULLARD TO MISS HUME.

I have been asked by your sister, Nurse Grace Hume, to hand the enclosed letter to you. My name is Nurse Mullard, and I was with your sister when she died. Our camp hospital at Vilvorde was burned to the ground, and out of 1,517 men and 23 nurses, only 19 nurses were saved, but 149 men managed to get away. Grace requested me to tell you that her last thoughts were of —— and you, and that you were not to worry over her, as she would be going to meet her Jack. These were her last words. She endured great agony in her last hours. One of the soldiers (our men) caught two German soldiers in the act of cutting off her left breast, her right one having been already cut off. They were killed instantly by our soldiers. Grace managed to scrawl the enclosed note before I found her, but we all say that your sister was a heroine. She was out on the fields looking for wounded soldiers, and on one occasion, when bringing in a wounded soldier, a German attacked her. She threw the soldier's gun at him and shot him with her rifle. Of course, all nurses here are armed. I have just received word this moment to pack to Scotland. Will try and get this handed to you, as there is no post from here, and we are making the best of a broken-down wagon truck for a shelter. Will give you fuller details when I see you. We are all quite safe now, as there have been reinforcements.

A condensed account appeared in the *Evening Standard* with the note : " This message has been submitted to the Press Bureau, which does not object to the publication and takes no responsibility for the correctness of the statement."

A story which attracted particular attention both because of its peculiar atrocity and because of the circumstantial details which accompanied it, was told in several of the evening papers on Wednesday. It was first published, we believe, in the *Dumfries Standard* on Wednesday morning and related to an English nurse, who was said to have been killed by Germans in Belgium with the most revolting cruelty. This nurse came from Dumfries and, according to the *Dumfries Standard*, the story was told to the nurse's sister in Dumfries by another nurse from Belgium, who also gave an account of it in a letter. Further, the *Dumfries Standard* published a facsimile of a letter said to have been written by the murdered nurse when dying to her sister in Dumfries. The story therefore appeared to be particularly well authenticated and, as we say, it was published by a number of London evening papers of repute, including the *Pall Mall* and *Westminster Gazette*, the *Globe*, the *Star*, and the *Evening Standard*. But late on Wednesday night it was discovered to be entirely untrue, since the nurse in question was actually in Huddersfield and had never been to Belgium, though she volunteered for the front. The remaining fact is that her sister in Dumfries states, according to the *Yorkshire Post*, that she was visited by a " Nurse Mullard," professing to be a nurse from Belgium, who told her the story and gave her the letter from her sister in a handwriting that resembled her sister's.

" Times " Leader, September 18, 1914.

The Times goes on to call for an inquiry and to suggest that the story may have been invented by German agents in order to discredit all atrocity stories.

Kate Hume, seventeen, was charged at Dumfries yesterday, before Sheriff Substitute Primrose, with having uttered a forged letter purporting to have been written by her sister, Nurse Grace Hume, in Huddersfield. She declined to make any statement, on the advice of her agent, and was committed to prison to await trial.

" The Times," September 30, 1914.

The case came before the High Court at Dumfries, and

it was proved that Kate Hume (the sister) had fabricated the whole story and forged both the letter from her sister and that from " Nurse Mullard " and had communicated them to the Press.

" The Times," December 29 and 30, 1914.

VII

THE CRIMINAL KAISER

HAVING declared the enemy the sole culprit and originator of the war, the next step is to personify the enemy. As a nation consists of millions of people and the absurd analogy of an individual criminal and a nation may become apparent even to moderately intelligent people, it is necessary to detach an individual on whom may be concentrated all the vials of the wrath of an innocent people who are only defending themselves from " unprovoked aggression." The sovereign is the obvious person to choose. While the Kaiser on many occasions, by his bluster and boasting, had been a subject of ridicule and offence, nevertheless, not many years before, his portrait had appeared in the *Daily Mail* with " A friend in need is a friend indeed " under it. And as late as October 17, 1913, the *Evening News* wrote :

> We all acknowledge the Kaiser as a very gallant gentleman whose word is better than many another's bond, a guest whom we are always glad to welcome and sorry to lose, a ruler whose ambitions for his own people are founded on as good right as our own.

When the signal was given, however, all this could be forgotten and the direct contrary line taken. The Kaiser turned out to be a most promising target for concentrated abuse. So successfully was it done that exaggeration soon became impossible; every crime in the calendar was laid at his door authoritatively, publicly and privately; and this was kept up all through the war. His past was reviewed, greatly to his discredit. Over his desire to fight Great Britain while we were engaged in the Boer War, however, there was an unfortunate contradiction in point of fact, as the following two extracts show :

Delcassé, with the help of the Czar, thrust aside German proposals for a Continental combination against us during the Boer War.
" The Times," October 14, 1915 (editorial on Delcassé's resignation).

At the time of the South African War, other nations were prepared to assist the Boers, but they stipulated that Germany should do likewise. The Kaiser refused.
General Botha, reported in the "Daily News," September 3, 1915.

But over his criminality in the Great War there was no difference of opinion.

He had called a secret Council of the Central Powers at Potsdam early in July 1914, at which it was decided to enforce war on Europe. This secret plot was first divulged by a Dutch newspaper in September 1914. The story was revived by The Times on July 28, 1917, and again in November 1919. It was believed even in Germany, until reports were received from various officers in touch with the Kaiser showing how he spent these days, and it was finally disposed of and proved to be a myth by the testimony of all those supposed to have taken part in it. This was in 1919, after the story had served its purpose.

Only a few of the thousand references to the Kaiser's personal criminality need be given.

He (the enemy) is beginning to realize the desperate character of the adventure on which the Kaiser embarked when he made this wanton war.
" Daily Mail," October 1, 1914.

The following letter from the late Sir W. B. Richmond, in the *Daily Mail* of September 22, 1914, is a forcibly expressed example of the accepted opinion :

Neither England nor civilized Europe and Asia is going to be set trembling by lunatic William, even though by his order Rheims Cathedral has been destroyed.

This last act of the barbarian chief will only draw us all closer together to be rid of a scourge the like of which the civilized world has never seen before.

The madman is piling up the logs of his own pyre. We can have no terror of the monster; we shall clench our teeth in determination that if we die to the last man the modern Judas and his hell-begotten brood shall be wiped out.

To achieve this righteous purpose we must be patient and plodding as well as energetic.

Our great England will shed its blood willingly to help rid civilization of a criminal monarch and a criminal court which have succeeded in creating out of a docile people a herd of savages.

Sir James Crichton Browne has said, in Dumfries : " A halter for the Kaiser " ; shooting him would be to give him the honourable death of a soldier. The halter is the shrift for this criminal.

Lord Robert Cecil said that for the terrible outrages, the wholesale breaches of every law and custom of civilized warfare which the Germans had committed, the people who were responsible were the German rulers, the Emperor and those who were closely advising him, and it was upon them, if possible, that our punishment and wrath should fall.

" The Times," May 15, 1915.

Cities have been burned, old men and children have been murdered, women and young girls have been outraged, harmless fishermen have been drowned, at this crowned criminal's orders. He will have to answer " at that great day when all the world is judged " for the victims of the *Falaba* and the *Lusitania*.

Leader on depriving the Kaiser of the Order of the Garter,
" Daily Express," May 14, 1915.

A *Punch* cartoon in 1918 depicted the Kaiser as Cain. Under it was put :

More than 14,000 non-combatants have been murdered by the Kaiser's orders.

There was a poster portrait of the Kaiser, his face composed of corpses, his mouth streaming with blood, which could be seen on the hoardings. The equivalent of this in France was "Guillaume le Boucher," the Kaiser in an apron with a huge knife dripping with blood. Throughout he was a good subject for the caricaturist, as he was so easy to draw.

The fiction having become popular and being universally accepted in the Allied countries, it became imperative for the Allied statesmen to insert a special clause in the Peace Treaty beginning :

The Allied and Associated Powers publicly arraign William II, of Hohenzollern, formerly German Emperor, for a supreme offence against international morality and the sanctity of treaties,

and going on to describe the constitution of "the special tribunal" before which he was to be tried.

Having committed themselves to the trial of the Kaiser by a clause in the Peace Treaty, the Allies were obliged to go through the formality of addressing a note to the Netherlands Government on January 16, 1920, dwelling on the Kaiser's "immense responsibility" and asking for him to be handed over "in order that he may be sent for trial." The refusal of the Netherlands Government on January 23rd was at once accepted and saved the Allied Governments from making hopeless fools of themselves. But before the decision was publicly known, and after it had been privately ascertained that the Government of Holland, whither the Kaiser had fled, would *not* give him up, the " Hang the Kaiser " campaign was launched, and in the General Election of 1918 candidates lost votes who would not commit themselves to this policy.

But the campaign had been launched before the decision of the Netherlands Government was made public.

The ruler (the Kaiser), who spoke for her pride and her majesty and her might for thirty years, is now a fugitive, soon to be placed on his trial (loud cheers) before the tribunals of lands which, on behalf of his country, he sought to intimidate.

Mr. Lloyd George, House of Commons, July 3, 1919.

. As a matter of fact, there was not the smallest intention of doing anything so absurd as try the Kaiser. Nor did anyone with knowledge of the facts believe him to be in any way personally responsible for starting the war. He was, and always had been, a tinsel figure-head of no account, with neither the courage to make a war nor the power to stop it.

His biographer, Emil Ludwig,[1] has written the most slashing indictment of William II that has appeared in any language, showing up his vanity, his megalomania, and his incompetence. But so far from accusing him of wanting or engineering the war, the author insists, time after time, on the Emperor's pacific attitude. " In all the European developments between 1908 and 1914, the Emperor was more pacific, was even more far-sighted, than his advisers." At the time of the Morocco crisis " the Emperor was peacefully inclined,"

[1] *Kaiser William II*, by Emil Ludwig.

and in the last days of July 1914, speaking of Germany, Austria, and Russia, Ludwig says :

Three Emperors avowedly opposed to war were driven by the ambition, vindictiveness, and incompetence of their Ministers into a conflict whose danger for their thrones they all three recognized from the first and, if only for that reason, tried to avoid.

Even Lord Grey says, now that it is all over :

If matters had rested with him (the Kaiser) there would have been no European War arising out of the Austro-Serbian dispute.

" Twenty-Five Years," vol. ii, p. 25.

Nevertheless, up to 1919 the Kaiser, as the villain of the piece, was set up in the Allied countries as the incarnation of all iniquity.

This very simple form of propaganda had a great influence on the people's feelings. There can be no question that thousands who joined up were under the impression that the primary object of the war was to catch this monster, little knowing that war is like chess : you cannot take the King while the game is going on; it is against the rules. It would spoil the game. In the same way G.H.Q. on both sides was never bombed because, as a soldier bluntly put it, " Don't you see, it would put an end to the whole bloody business."

Finding he had unfortunately not been caught or killed during the war, the people put their faith in his being tried and hanged when the war was over. If he was all that had been described to them, this was the least that could be expected.

When, as months and years passed, it was discovered that no responsible person really believed, or had ever believed, in his personal guilt, that the cry, " Hang the

Kaiser," was a piece of deliberate bluff, and that when all was over and millions of innocent people had been killed, he, the criminal, the monster, the plotter and initiator of the whole catastrophe, was allowed to live comfortably and peacefully in Holland, the disillusionment to simple, uninformed people was far greater than was ever realized. It was the exposure of this crude falsehood that first led many humble individuals to inquire whether, in other connections, they had not also been duped.

VIII

THE BELGIAN BABY WITHOUT HANDS

Not only did the Belgian baby whose hands had been cut off by the Germans travel through the towns and villages of Great Britain, but it went through Western Europe and America, even into the Far West. No one paused to ask how long a baby would live were its hands cut off unless expert surgical aid were at hand to tie up the arteries (the answer being, a very few minutes). Everyone wanted to believe the story, and many went so far as to say they had seen the baby. The lie was as universally accepted as the passage of the Russian troops through Britain.

One man whom I did not see told an official of the Catholic Society that he had seen with his own eyes German soldiery chop off the arms of a baby which clung to its mother's skirts.
"The Times" Correspondent in Paris, August 27, 1914.

On September 2, 1914, *The Times* Correspondent quotes French refugees declaring: " They cut the hands off the little boys so that there shall be no more soldiers for France."

Pictures of the baby without hands were very popular on the Continent, both in France and in Italy. *Le Rive Rouge* had a picture on September 18, 1915, and on July 26, 1916, made it still more lurid by depicting German soldiers eating the hands. *Le Journal* gave, on April 30, 1915, a photograph of a statue of a child without hands. But the most savage of all, which

contained in it no elements of caricature, was issued by
the Allies for propaganda purposes and published in
Critica, in Buenos Ayres (reproduced in the *Sphere,*
January 30, 1925). The heading of the picture was,
" The Bible before All," and under it was written :
" Suffer little children to come unto Me." The Kaiser
is depicted standing behind a huge block with an axe,
his hands darkly stained with blood. Round the block
are piles of hands. He is beckoning to a woman to
bring a number of children, who are clinging to her,
some having had their hands cut off already.

Babies not only had their hands cut off, but they were
impaled on bayonets, and in one case nailed to a door.
But everyone will remember the handless Belgian baby.
It was loudly spoken of in buses and other public
places, had been seen in a hospital, was now in the next
parish, etc., and it was paraded, not as an isolated
instance of an atrocity, but as a typical instance of a
common practice.

In Parliament there was the usual evasion, which
suggested the story was true, although the only evidence
given was " seen by witnesses."

Mr. A. K. Lloyd asked the First Lord of the Treasury
whether materials are available for identifying and tracing
the survivors of those children whose hands were cut off
by the Germans, and whose cases are referred to by letter
and number in the Report of the Bryce Committee ; and, if
so, whether he will consider the possibility of making the
information accessible, confidentially or otherwise, to persons
interested in the future of these survivors ?

Sir G. Cave : My Right Hon. Friend has asked me to
reply to this question. In all but two of the individual
cases in which children were seen by witnesses mutilated in
this manner, the child was either dead or dying from the
treatment it had received. In view of the fact that these

children were in Belgium, which is still in German occupation, it is unlikely that they could now be traced, and any attempt to do so at this time might lead to the further persecution of the victims or their relatives.

MR. LLOYD : Were there not other cases brought over here to hospital ?

SIR G. CAVE : Not the cases to which the Hon. Member's question refers.

House of Commons, December 19, 1916.

Sometimes the handless person was grown up. A Mr. Tyler, at a Brotherhood meeting in Glasgow on April 17, 1915, said he had a friend in Harrogate who had seen a nurse with both her hands cut off by Germans. He gave the address of his informant. A letter was at once addressed to the friend at Harrogate, asking if the statement was correct, but no reply was ever received.

But the most harrowing and artistically dressed version of the handless child story appeared in the *Sunday Chronicle* on May 2, 1915.

Some days ago a charitable great lady was visiting a building in Paris where have been housed for several months a number of Belgian refugees. During her visit she noticed a child, a girl of ten, who, though the room was hot rather than otherwise, kept her hands in a pitiful little worn muff. Suddenly the child said to the mother : " Mamma, please blow my nose for me." " Shocking," said the charitable lady, half-laughing, half-severe, " a big girl like you, who can't use her own handkerchief." The child said nothing, and the mother spoke in a dull, matter-of-fact tone. " She has not any hands now, ma'am," she said.

The grand dame looked, shuddered, understood. " Can it be," she said, " that the Germans——? " The mother burst into tears. That was her answer.

Signor Nitti, who was Italian Prime Minister during the war, states in his memoirs :

THE BELGIAN BABY WITHOUT HANDS

To bring the truth of the present European crisis home to the world it is necessary to destroy again and again the vicious legends created by war propaganda. During the war France, in common with other Allies, including our own Government in Italy, circulated the most absurd inventions to arouse the fighting spirit of our people. The cruelties attributed to the Germans were such as to curdle our blood. We heard the story of poor little Belgian children whose hands were cut off by the Huns. After the war a rich American, who was deeply touched by the French propaganda, sent an emissary to Belgium with the intention of providing a livelihood for the children whose poor little hands had been cut off. He was unable to discover one. Mr. Lloyd George and myself, when at the head of the Italian Government, carried on extensive investigations as to the truth of these horrible accusations, some of which, at least, were told specifically as to names and places. Every case investigated proved to be a myth.

Colonel Repington, in his *Diary of the World War*, vol. ii, p. 447, says :

I was told by Cardinal Gasquet that the Pope promised to make a great protest to the world if a single case could be proved of the violation of Belgian nuns or cutting off of children's hands. An inquiry was instituted and many cases examined with the help of the Belgian Cardinal Mercier. Not one case could be proved.

The former French Minister of Finance, Klotz, to whom at the beginning of the war the censorship of the Press was entrusted, says, in his memoirs (*De la Guerre à la Paix*, Paris, Payot, 1924) :

One evening I was shown a proof of the *Figaro*, in which two scientists of repute asserted and endorsed by their signatures that they had seen with their own eyes about a hundred children whose hands had been chopped off by the Germans.

F

In spite of the evidence of these scientists I entertained doubts as to the accuracy of the report and forbade the publication of it. When the editor of the *Figaro* expressed his indignation, I declared myself ready to investigate, in the presence of the American Ambassador, the matter that would stir the world. I required, however, that the name of the place where these investigations had to take place should be given by the two scientists. I insisted on having these details supplied immediately. I am still without their reply or visit.

But this lie obtained such a hold on people's imagination that it is by no means dead yet. Quite recently a Liverpool poet, in a volume called *A Medley of Song*, has written the following lines in a " patriotic " poem :

> They stemmed the first mad onrush
> Of the cultured German Hun,
> Who'd outraged every female Belgian
> And maimed every mother's son.

IX

THE LOUVAIN ALTAR-PIECE

At the Peace Conference the Belgian representatives claimed the wings of Dietrick Bouts's altar-piece in compensation for the famous altar-piece from Louvain, a valuable work of art which they declared had been wantonly thrown into the flames of the burning library by a German officer. The story was accepted and the two pictures transferred. But it was not true.

The *New Statesman* of April 12, 1924, gives the facts :

The Dietrick Bouts altar-piece was not thrown into the flames by the Germans or by anyone else. The picture is still in existence at Louvain, perfectly intact, and the Germans were not its destroyers but its preservers. A German officer saved it from the flames and gave it to the burgomaster, who had it taken for safe custody to the vaults of the Town Hall and walled in there. It has been duly unwalled. . . .

X

THE CONTEMPTIBLE LITTLE ARMY

THERE can be no question that the most successful slogan for recruiting purposes issued during the whole course of the war was the phrase " the contemptible little army," said to have been used by the Kaiser in reference to the British Expeditionary Force. It very naturally created a passionate feeling of resentment throughout the country. The history of this lie and of its exposure is extremely interesting.

In an annexe to B.E.F. Routine Orders of September 24, 1914, the following was issued :

The following is a copy of Orders issued by the German Emperor on August 19th:

" It is my Royal and Imperial command that you con-centrate your energies for the immediate present upon one single purpose, and that is that you address all your skill and all the valour of my soldiers to exterminate first, the treacherous English, walk over General French's con-temptible little army. . . .

" HEADQUARTERS, AIX LA CHAPELLE, *August 19th*."

The results of the order were the operations commencing with Mons, and the advance of the seemingly overwhelming masses against us. The answer of the British Army on the subject of extermination has already been given.

Printing Co., R.E.69.

The authenticity of this official military declaration was naturally never questioned, although one attempt was made to pretend that it was an incorrect translation.

The indignation roused throughout the country was heartfelt and widespread.

The Times Military Correspondent referred to the Kaiser as being in "a high state of agitation and excitability," and the leader-writer in *The Times* (October 1, 1914), referring to the statement, said:

> In spite of the ferocious order of the Kaiser . . . to-day.
> "French's contemptible little army" is not yet exterminated.

On the same day *The Times* printed a poem entitled "French's Contemptible Little Army."

> The Kaiser scoffed at the British Army and labelled it "contemptible" because it was small. He felt grossly insulted that any army that did not count its men in millions should dare to assail the might of the Hohenzollerns, and against this small British David, in a pronouncement which will certainly be historic, he directed his Goliath legions to "concentrate their energies."
>
> *"Daily Express," October 2, 1914.*

Mr. Churchill made great play with it in a recruiting speech at the London Opera House on September 11, 1914.

In March 1915 *Punch* had a cartoon of the German Eagle in conversation with the Kaiser: "It's like this, then; you told me the British Lion was contemptible —well—he wasn't."

And again, in 1917 (after the entry of America into the war), a cartoon depicted the Crown Prince saying to the Kaiser (who is drafting his next speech): "For Gott's sake, father, be careful and don't call the American Army 'contemptible'!"

There was not a village in the land where the expression was not known and not a provincial newspaper in which it was not quoted, until at last the word was used as the designation of the officers and men who were in the original Expeditionary Force. They became known as " the old Contemptibles."

A thorough investigation of the authenticity of this order, " issued by the Kaiser," was undertaken in 1925 with the assistance of a German General, who had the archives in Berlin carefully searched, and of a British General, Sir F. Maurice, who was able to throw a good deal of light on the subject.

While the Kaiser's proverbially foolish indiscretion might account for any preposterous utterance, it was known that he did not issue orders of his own volition ; they were prepared for him by his Staff, which was certainly not so ignorant of its business as to tell the German Generals to concentrate their energies upon the extermination of an army when they could not tell them where that army was. Their ignorance of the whereabouts of the British Army was proved by a telegram sent by the German Chief of the Staff to Von Kluck on August 20th (the day after the issue of the supposed order) : " Disembarkation of English at Boulogne must be reckoned with. The opinion here, however, is that large disembarkations have not yet taken place."

It was further discovered that German Headquarters were never at Aix la Chapelle. Headquarters moved from Berlin about August 15th and went to Coblenz, later to Luxemburg, from whence they moved to Charleville on September 27th.

A careful search in the archives proved fruitless. No such order or anything like it could be discovered. Not content with this, however, the German General had inquiries made of the ex-Kaiser himself at Doorn. In a marginal note the ex-Kaiser declared he had never used such an expression, adding : " On the contrary, I continually emphasized the high value of the British Army, and often, indeed, in peace-time gave warning against underestimating it."

General Sir F. Maurice had the German newspaper files searched for the alleged speech or order of the Kaiser, but without success.   In an article exposing the fabrication (*Daily News*, November 6, 1925), he remarks that G.H.Q. hit on the idea of using routine orders to issue statements which it was believed would encourage and inspirit our men.   " Most of these took the form of casting ridicule on the German Army. . . . These efforts were seen to be absurd by the men in the trenches, and were soon dropped."

We may laugh now at this lie and some may be inclined to give some credit to the officer who con-cocted it, although he made a careless mistake about the whereabouts of the German G.H.Q.   There can be no doubt as to its immense success, nevertheless there are many who will share the opinion of a gentleman who wrote to the Press (*Nation and Athenæum*, August 8, 1925), who, having heard that doubt was cast on the authenticity of the well-known and almost hackneyed phrase, remarked on " its extreme seriousness to our national honour or to that of the British officer originally responsible," were it proved to be an invention.

XI

DEUTSCHLAND ÜBER ALLES

A GREAT deal of play was made throughout the war with the opening lines of a German patriotic song.

"Deutschland über Alles auf der ganzen Welt."
("Germany above all things in the whole world.")

There must have been many people who knew sufficient German to understand the meaning of the phrase, but no protest was made at the mistranslation, which was habitually used to illustrate Germany's aggressive imperialist ambitions. It was popularly accepted as meaning, "(Let) Germany (rule) over everywhere in the whole world," i.e. the German domination of the world.

Mr. Lloyd George used it on September 20, 1914, at Queen's Hall :

Treaties are gone, the honour of nations gone, liberty gone. What is left ? Germany, Germany is left.
Deutschland über Alles.

Punch kept it to the front in various cartoons.

The Kaiser, playing on a flute, having abandoned a broken big drum labelled " Deutschland über Alles."
The Kaiser trying to blow up a pricked balloon labelled " Deutschland über Alles."
The Kaiser as the High Priest of Moloch. Moloch labelled " Deutschland über Alles."

It was constantly quoted in numberless articles in the Press. When a prominent Member of Parliament used the expression in a letter to *The Times*, the incorrect meaning he attributed to it was pointed out to him. He admitted the error, but seemed to consider that the accepted meaning of it justified his using it as he did.

The false meaning spread through the country and the Empire, and the Department of Education in Ontario went so far as to order the song to be eliminated from German school books throughout the province (*The Times*, March 19, 1915).

Even after the war, in November 1921, a leader-writer in a prominent newspaper declared that as long as the Germans stuck to their national anthem, " Deutschland über Alles auf der ganzen Welt," there would be no peace in Europe.

XII

THE BABY OF COURBECK LOO

IT is not often that we have a confession of falsehood, but the story of the baby of Courbeck Loo is an illuminating example of an invention related by its author.

Captain F. W. Wilson, formerly editor of the *Sunday Times*, related the story in America in 1922. The following account appeared in the *New York Times* (reproduced in the *Crusader*, February 24, 1922):

A correspondent of the London *Daily Mail*, Captain Wilson, found himself in Brussels at the time the war broke out. They telegraphed out that they wanted stories of atrocities. Well, there weren't any atrocities at that time. So then they telegraphed out that they wanted stories of refugees. So I said to myself, " That's fine, I won't have to move." There was a little town outside Brussels where one went to get dinner—a very good dinner, too. I heard the Hun had been there. I supposed there must have been a baby there. So I wrote a heart-rending story about the baby of Courbeck Loo being rescued from the Hun in the light of the burning homesteads.

The next day they telegraphed out to me to send the baby along, as they had about five thousand letters offering to adopt it. The day after that baby clothes began to pour into the office. Even Queen Alexandra wired her sympathy and sent some clothes. Well, I couldn't wire ba k to them that there wasn't a baby. So I finally arranged with the doctor that took care of the refugees that the blessed baby died of some very contagious disease, so it couldn't even have a public burial.

And we got Lady Northcliffe to start a crêche with all the baby-clothes.

XIII

THE CRUCIFIED CANADIAN

LIKE so many other stories, this one underwent considerable changes and variations. The crucified person was at one time a girl, at another an American, but most often a Canadian.

Last week a large number of Canadian soldiers, wounded in the fighting round Ypres, arrived at the base hospital at Versculles. They all, told a story of how one of their officers had been crucified by the Germans. He had been pinned to a wall by bayonets thrust through his hands and feet, another bayonet had then been driven through his throat, and, finally, he was riddled with bullets. The wounded Canadians said that the Dublin Fusiliers had seen this done with their own eyes, and they had heard the officers of the Dublin Fusiliers talking about it.

" *The Times,*" *May* 10, 1915. *Paris Correspondent.*

There is, unhappily, good reason to believe that the story related by your Paris Correspondent of the crucifixion of a Canadian officer during the fighting at Ypres on April 22, 1923, is in substance true. The story was current here at the time, but, in the absence of direct evidence and absolute proof, men were unwilling to believe that a civilized foe could be guilty of an act so cruel and savage.

Now, I have reason to believe, written depositions testifying to the fact of the discovery of the body are in possession of British Headquarters Staff.

The unfortunate victim was a sergeant. As the story was told to me, he was found transfixed to the wooden fence of a farm building. Bayonets were thrust through the palms of his hands and his feet, pinning him to the fence. He had been repeatedly stabbed with bayonets, and there were many punctured wounds in his body.

I have not heard that any of our men actually saw the crime committed. There is room for the supposition that the man was dead before he was pinned to the fence and that the enemy, in his insensate rage and hate of the English, wreaked his vengeance on the lifeless body of his foe. That is the most charitable complexion that can be put on the deed, ghastly as it is.

There is not a man in the ranks of the Canadians who fought at Ypres who is not firmly convinced that this vile thing has been done. They know, too, that the enemy bayoneted their wounded and helpless comrades in the trenches.

" The Times," May 15, 1915. Correspondent, North France.

MR. HOUSTON asked the Under-Secretary of State for War whether he has any information regarding the crucifixion of three Canadian soldiers recently captured by the Germans, who nailed them with bayonets to the side of a wooden structure.

MR. TENNANT : No, sir; no information of such an atrocity having been perpetrated has yet reached the War Office.

MR. HOUSTON : Is the Right Hon. Gentleman aware that Canadian officers and Canadian soldiers who were eyewitnesses of these fiendish outrages have made affidavits ? Has the officer in command at the base at Boulogne not called the attention of the War Office to them ?

MR. HARCOURT : No, sir; we have no record of it.

House of Commons, May 12, 1915.

Mr. HOUSTON asked the Under-Secretary of State for War whether he has any official information showing that during the recent fighting, when the Canadians were temporarily driven back, they were compelled to leave about forty of their wounded comrades in a barn, and that on recapturing the position they found the Germans had bayoneted all the wounded with the exception of a sergeant, and that the Germans had removed the figure of Christ from the large village crucifix and fastened the sergeant, while alive, to the cross ; and whether he is aware that the crucifixion of our soldiers is becoming a practice of Germans.

MR. TENNANT : The military authorities in France have

standing instructions to send particulars of any authenticated cases of atrocities committed against our troops by the Germans. No official information in the sense of the Hon. Member's question has been received, but, owing to the information conveyed by the Hon. Member's previous question, inquiry is being made and is not yet complete.

House of Commons, May 19, 1915.

The story went the round of the Press here and in Canada, and was used by Members of Parliament on the platform. Its authenticity, however, was eventually denied by General March at Washington.

It cropped up again in 1919, when a letter was published by the *Nation* (April 12th) from Private E. Loader, 2nd Royal West Kent Regiment, who declared he had seen the crucified Canadian. The *Nation* was informed in a subsequent letter from Captain E. N. Bennett that there was no such private on the rolls of the Royal West Kents, and that the 2nd Battalion was in India during the whole war.[1]

[1] For the American version see p. 184.

XIV

THE SHOOTING OF THE FRANZÖSLING

THIS is one of the lies which arose from a mistranslation. On September 30, 1914, a communication was issued by the Press Bureau, which was published by *The Times* the following day. It was said to be a copy of the *Kriegschronik* " seized by the Custom House authorities at ports of landing." The extract given was as follows :

A traitor has just been shot (in the Vosges), a little French lad (*ein Französling*) belonging to one of those gymnastic societies which wear tricolour ribbons (i.e. the Éclaireurs, or Boy Scouts), a poor young fellow who, in his infatuation, wanted to be a hero. The German column was passing along a wooded defile, and he was caught and asked whether the French were about. He refused to give information. Fifty yards further on there was fire from the cover of a wood. The prisoner was asked in French if he had known that the enemy was in the forest, and did not deny it. He went with a firm step to a telegraph post and stood up against it, with the green vineyard at his back, and received the volley of the firing party with a proud smile on his face. Infatuated wretch ! It was a pity to see such wasted courage.

Mr. J. A. Hobson wrote, in *The Times* of October 5, 1914, to point out an inaccuracy in the account of German atrocities issued by the Press Bureau and published by *The Times*.

The passage describes how " a little French lad (*ein Französling*) " was shot for refusing to disclose the proximity of some French soldiers. The word " Französling," Mr. Hobson wrote, " does not mean a little

French boy," but is "used exclusively to describe German subjects with French proclivities. In Alsace and Lorraine there exist societies of these Französlings, who wear the French colours. They are not boys but grown men."

"Constant Reader" wrote to *The Times* on October 6, 1914:

You publish on page 6 of your issue of this morning a note communicated by a Mr. J. A. Hobson, which insinuates that the young victim of a German firing party in the Vosges, whose fate was described in a German soldier's letter printed last week, may have been a " grown man " and not a " lad." At least, Mr. Hobson says that " The societies of these Französlings who wear the French colours are not boys but grown men." But he has evidently not seen the original letter, which calls the victim an *armer junger Kerl*—a poor lad; and a *junger Verräter*—a young traitor. Moreover, it is clear that if this had been a grown man of military age, he would have been doing military service and not have been at large upon the roads.

This letter must have been from the Press Bureau, as *The Times* original note made no reference to its being from a German soldier's letter, nor quoted the German text. "Constant Reader" had evidently been reading elsewhere.

Mr. J. A. Hobson wrote to *The Times* on October 8, 1914:

In reply to " Constant Reader," may I point out that the object of my note upon the " Französling " incident was to state that the word meant a " pro-French German " and not, as translated by the Press Bureau, " a little French lad "? That he was " a young fellow " is not in dispute, but that affords no justification for calling him a " Boy Scout."

It does not seem to have been pointed out that no

body of Boy Scouts called Éclaireurs, and wearing tricolour ribbons, could have existed in *German* Alsace.

The Press Bureau tells us that an official paper circulated among the German troops chuckled with satisfaction at the killing of a French boy who refused to divulge to the enemy the whereabouts of French forces.

"*Daily Express*," *October*, 1914.

The Press Bureau story headed " Little French Hero " was printed in the same issue. The whole object of the Press Bureau was to incense public opinion against the Germans for shooting *a boy*. The shooting of spies was not condemned, as *The Times* itself reported also from the Vosges that

Germans caught red-handed in acts of espionage were court-marshalled. Among others were the mayor and postmaster of Thann, who were shot.

People may be further mystified in looking up this case by finding it in *The Times* index under the heading " Shooting of Franz Ösling."

XV

LITTLE ALF'S STAMP COLLECTION

A CLERGYMAN, while lunching in a restaurant in 1918, was informed by a stranger that the son of a friend of his was interned in a camp in Germany. A recent letter, he said, had contained the passage, "The stamp on this letter is a rare one; soak it off for little Alf's collection." Though there was no one in the family called Alf, and no one who collected stamps, they did as they were told. Underneath the stamp were the words, "They have torn out my tongue; I could not put it in the letter" (the news presumably, not the tongue). The clergyman told the man the story was absurd, and that he ought to be ashamed of himself for repeating it, as everyone knew that prisoners' letters did not bear stamps. If his friend had managed to put a stamp on his letter, it was the best possible way of attracting attention to what he was trying to hide. But the stranger, no doubt from patriotic motives, indignantly refused to have his story spoiled, and it was widely circulated in Manchester.[1]

The interesting point about this lie is that it was also used in Germany with variations. A lady in Munich received a letter from her son, who was a prisoner in Russia. He told her to take the stamp off his letter "as it was a rare one." She did so, and discovered written underneath, "They have cut off both my feet, so that I cannot escape." The story was eventually killed

---

[1] " Artifex," in the *Manchester Guardian*.

G

by ridicule, but not before it had travelled to Augsburg and other towns.

It was probably one of the stories which are used in every war.

XVI

THE TATTOOED MAN

Towards the end of 1918 a statement was circulated, supported by photographs, that English prisoners had been tattooed with the German Eagle, a cobra, or other devices on their faces. The interesting feature in this lie is that it seems to have emanated from quite a number of different individuals, each one eager to embroider some entirely unsubstantiated rumour which had spread.

Tattooing Charges not Confirmed.

On December 7th a statement appeared in the Press that a ship's fireman named Burton Mayberry had arrived at Newcastle bearing on his cheeks tattoo marks representing heads of cobras, which he alleged had been inflicted by two sailors by order of a German submarine commander in mid-Atlantic, on the occasion of the torpedoing of Mayberry's ship in April 1917. Pictures of Mayberry, showing the head of a cobra on each cheek, have also appeared in various illustrated papers.

The matter has been investigated, and it has been ascertained that on November 13th Mayberry applied for registration as a seaman preparatory to offering himself for employment in the British mercantile marine, and that, in making his application, he stated that he had had no previous sea service. He has now disappeared, and it seems that his disappearance took place after receiving a request to attend in order to receive his registration certificate. Former associates of Mayberry state that he never made any allusion to the alleged outrage.

Frequent statements have recently appeared in the Press with regard to the alleged branding of British soldiers by

the Germans, but the responsible authorities have been
unable to obtain any confirmation of these allegations.
"The Times," December 23, 1918.

The following extract from the *Manchester Guardian*
and the statement of " Artifex " (the pseudonym of a
well-known Manchester ecclesiastic) give other versions
of the story more fully.

Our contributor " Artifex " ventured to suggest last
week that the story of the prisoner who had been tattooed
on the cheek by ·the Germans, which had gained through a
section of the Press a wide currency among simple people,
was not established by any credible evidence. He tells us
to-day that he has since been deluged with letters enclosing
accounts of just how the man was tattooed, and giving
details of his former history and of his present occupation
and domestic relations. Each of the correspondents who
sent these letters was no doubt confirmed, by the cutting he
sent, in his belief in the truth of the tale and in the wilful
blindness of " Artifex." Unfortunately for their authors,
the stories vary so profoundly in essential facts as to make
it clear to anyone who correlates them, as " Artifex " has
done, that they are born of a myth, rapidly spread, and
gathering variety as it goes. If that were not enough,
there is yet more irrefutable evidence. The camera, it is
said, cannot lie. Yet on December 9th two different newspapers published photographs of the victim. Each picture
represents his whole right profile. The one shows his
cheek marked with a full-length snake, in black, the other
decorates it with a snake's head in outline. But a tattoo is
a permanent mark which years cannot alter or deface. Any
jury confronted with these conflicting pictures would be
forced to agree that the disfigurement was daily reapplied
by the sufferer, and that he had omitted the precaution of
having the same device repeated. Now this story must
have added vastly to the anxieties of many families who
have prisoners in enemy hands. Early in the war the
authorities did not hesitate to recommend the suppression
of the many reports of chivalrous treatment of our soldiers

by the Turks. That, in the light of the Turkish Government's record as a whole, may have been reasonable. But we suggest that they should be at least not less active to prevent the spread of stories about the treatment of our prisoners which are as dubious as this one.

" Manchester Guardian," *December* 19, 1918.

Extract from " Artifex " comments :

Not indeed that I ought to complain, in this case, of lack of corroborative evidence. I have been assured that the man, while working in a dockyard on the Tyne, has also (1) undergone skin-grafting in Salford Royal Hospital, (2) gone mad with horror in Leaf Square Hospital, (3) caused by his awful appearance the premature confinement and death of his young wife at Levenshulme, (4) thrown his delicate twelve-year-old daughter into fits at Stockport, (5) lived for nine months in a house in Weaste without ever coming out except after dark, which is why none of the neighbours have ever seen him, and (6) resided for the whole time also at Gorton, Swinton, Pendlebury and Tyldesley.

XVII

THE CORPSE FACTORY

A SERIES of extracts will give the record of one of the most revolting lies invented during the war, the dissemination of which throughout not only this country but the world was encouraged and connived at by both the Government and the Press. It started in 1917, and was not finally disposed of till 1925.

(Most of the quotations given are from *The Times*. The references in the lower strata of the Press, it will be remembered, were far more lurid.)

One of the United States consuls, on leaving Germany in February 1917, stated in Switzerland that the Germans were distilling glycerine from the bodies of their dead.
                                    " The Times," April 16, 1917.

Herr Karl Rosner, the Correspondent of the Berlin *Lokalanzeiger*, on the Western front . . . published last Tuesday the first definite German admission concerning the way in which the Germans use dead bodies.
We pass through Everingcourt. There is a dull smell in the air as if lime were being burnt. We are passing the great Corpse Exploitation Establishment (*Kadaververwertungs-anstalt*) of this Army Group. The fat that is won here is turned into lubricating oils, and everything else is ground down in the bone mill into a powder which is used for mixing with pig's food and as manure—nothing can be permitted to go to waste.
                                    " The Times," April 16, 1917.

There was a report in *The Times* of April 17, 1917, from *La Belgique* (Leyden), via *l'Indépendance Belge*, for April 10, giving a very long and detailed account of a

Deutsche Abfallverwertungs-gesellschaft factory near
Coblenz, where train-loads of the stripped bodies of
German soldiers, wired into bundles, arrive and are
simmered down in cauldrons, the products being
stearine and refined oil.

In *The Times* of April 18, 1917, there was a letter
from C. E. Bunbury commenting and suggesting the
use of the story for propaganda purposes, in neutral
countries and the East, where it would be especially
calculated to horrify Buddhists, Hindus, and Mohammedans. He suggested broadcasting by the Foreign
Office, India Office, and Colonial Office ; there were
other letters to the same effect on April 19th.

In *The Times* of April 20, 1917, there was a story told
by Sergeant B——, of the Kents, that a prisoner had
told him that the Germans boil down their dead for
munitions and pig and poultry food. " This fellow
told me that Fritz calls his margarine ' corpse fat '
because they suspect that's what it comes from."

The Times stated that it had received a number of
letters "questioning the translation of the German
word *Kadaver*, and suggesting that it is not used of
human bodies. As to this, the best authorities are
agreed that it is also used of the bodies of animals."
Other letters were received confirming the story from
Belgian and Dutch sources (later from Roumania).

There was an article in the *Lancet* discussing the
" business aspect " (or rather the technical one) of
the industry. An expression of horror appeared from
the Chinese Minister in London, and also from the
Maharajah of Bikanir, in *The Times* of April 21, 1917.

The Times of April 23, 1917, quotes a German statement that the report is " loathsome and ridiculous,"
and that *Kadaver* is never used of a human body. *The*

Times produces dictionary quotations to show that it is. Also that both *Tierkörpermehl* and *Kadavermehl* appear in German official catalogues, the implication being that they must be something different.

In *The Times* of April 24, 1917, there was a letter, signed E. H. Parker, enclosing copy of the *North China Herald*, March 3, 1917, recounting an interview between the German Minister and the Chinese Premier in Pekin :

But the matter was clinched when Admiral von Hinke was dilating upon the ingenious methods by which German scientists were obtaining chemicals necessary for the manufacture of munitions. The admiral triumphantly stated that they were extracting glycerine out of their dead soldiers ! From that moment onward the horrified Premier had no more use for Germany, and the business of persuading him to turn against her became comparatively easy.

The following questions in Parliament show the Government evading the issue, although they knew there was not a particle of authentic evidence for the report—a good instance of the official method of spreading falsehood.

MR. RONALD MCNEILL asked the Prime Minister if he will take steps to make it known as widely as possible in Egypt, India, and the East generally, that the Germans use the dead bodies of their own soldiers and of their enemies when they obtain possession of them, as food for swine.

MR. DILLON asked the Chancellor of the Exchequer whether his attention has been called to the reports widely circulated in this country that the German Government have set up factories for extracting fat from the bodies of soldiers killed in battle ; whether these reports have been endorsed by many prominent men in this country, including Lord Curzon of Kedleston ; whether the Government have any solid grounds for believing that these statements are well-founded ; and if so, whether he will communicate the information at the disposal of the Government to the House.

LORD R. CECIL: With respect to this question and that standing in the name of the Hon. Member for East Mayo, the Government have no information at present beyond that contained in extracts from the German Press which have been published in the Press here. In view of other actions by German military authorities, there is nothing incredible in the present charge against them. His Majesty's Government have allowed the circulation of facts as they have appeared through the usual channels.

MR. McNEILL: Can the Right Hon. Gentleman answer whether the Government will take any steps to give wide publicity in the East to this story emanating from German sources?

LORD R. CECIL: I think at present it is not desirable to take any other steps than those that have been taken.

MR. DILLON: May I ask whether we are to conclude from that answer that the Government have no solid evidence whatever in proof of the truth of this charge, and they have taken no steps to investigate it; and has their attention been turned to the fact that it is not only a gross scandal, but a very great evil to this country to allow the circulation of such statements, authorized by Ministers of the Crown, if they are, as I believe them to be, absolutely false?

LORD R. CECIL: The Hon. Member has, perhaps, information that we have not. I can only speak from statements that have been published in the Press. I have already told the House that we have no other information whatever. The information is the statement that has been published and that I have before me (quoting *Times* quotation from *Lokalanzeiger*). This statement has been published in the Press, and that is the whole of the information that I have.

MR. DILLON: Has the Noble Lord's attention been drawn to the fact that there have been published in the *Frankfurter Zeitung* and other leading German newspapers descriptions of this whole process, in which the word *Kadaver* is used, and from which it is perfectly manifest that these factories are for the purpose of boiling down the dead bodies of horses and other animals which are lying on the battlefield—(an

HON. MEMBER : " Human animals ! ")—and I ask the Right Hon. Gentleman whether the Government propose to take any steps to obtain authentic information whether this story that has been circulated is true or absolutely false. For the credit of human nature, he ought to.

LORD R. CECIL : It is not any part of the duties of the Government, nor is it possible for the Government, to institute inquiries as to what goes on in Germany. The Hon. Member is surely very unreasonable in making the suggestion, and as for his quotations from the *Frankfurter Zeitung*, I have not seen them, but I have seen statements made by the German Government after the publication of this, and I confess that I am not able to attach very great importance to any statements made by the German Government.

MR. DILLON : I beg to ask the Right Hon. Gentleman whether, before a Minister of the Crown, a member of the War Cabinet, gives authorization to these rumours, he ought not to have obtained accurate information as to whether they are true or not.

LORD R. CECIL : I think any Minister of the Crown is entitled to comment on and refer to something which has been published in one of the leading papers of the country. He only purported to do that, and did not make himself responsible for the statement (an HON. MEMBER : " He did ! "). I am informed that he did not. He said : " As has been stated in the papers."

MR. OUTHWAITE : May I ask if the Noble Lord is aware that the circulation of these reports (interruption) has caused anxiety and misery to British people who have lost their sons on the battlefield, and who think that their bodies may be put to this purpose, and does not that give a reason why he should try to find out the truth of what is happening in Germany ?

House of Commons, April 30, 1917.

In *The Times* of May 3, 1917, there were quotations from the *Frankfurter Zeitung* stating that the French Press is now treating the *Kadaver* story as a " misunderstanding."

The Times of May 17, 1917, reported that Herr Zimmermann denied in the Reichstag that human bodies were used; and stated that the story appeared first in the French Press.

In reply to a question in the House of Commons on May 23rd, Mr. A. Chamberlain stated that the report would be " available to the public in India through the usual channels."

A corpse factory cartoon appeared in *Punch*.

KAISER (to 1917 recruit): And don't forget that your Kaiser will find a use for you alive or dead. (At the enemy's establishment for the utilization of corpses the dead bodies of German soldiers are treated chemically, the chief commercial products being lubricant oils and pig food.)

View of the corpse factory out of the window.

The story had a world-wide circulation and had considerable propaganda value in the East. Not till 1925 did the truth emerge.

A painful impression has been produced here by an unfortunate speech of Brigadier-General Charteris at the dinner of the National Arts Club, in which he professed to tell the true story of the war-time report that Germany was boiling down the bodies of her dead soldiers in order to get fats for munitions and fertilizers.

According to General Charteris, the story began as propaganda for China. By transposing the caption from one of two photographs found on German prisoners to the other he gave the impression that the Germans were making a dreadful use of their own dead soldiers. This photograph he sent to a Chinese newspaper in Shanghai. He told the familiar story of its later republication in England and of the discussion it created there. He told, too, how, when a question put in the House was referred to him, he answered it by saying that from what he knew of German mentality, he was prepared for anything.

Later, said General Charteris, in order to support the story, what purported to be the diary of a German soldier was forged in his office. It was planned to have this discovered on a dead German by a war correspondent with a passion for German diaries, but the plan was never carried out. The diary was now in the war museum in London.

"*The Times,*" *October 22, 1925. From New York Correspondent.*

Some opinions of politicians may be given.

LLOYD GEORGE : The story came under my notice in various ways at the time. I did not believe it then ; I do not believe it now. It was never adopted as part of the armoury of the British Propaganda Department. It was, in fact, " turned down " by that department.

MR. MASTERMAN : We certainly did not accept the story as true, and I know nobody in official positions at the time who credited it. Nothing as suspect as this was made use of in our propaganda. Only such information as had been properly verified was circulated.

MR. I. MACPHERSON : I was at the War Office at the time. We had no reason to doubt the authenticity of the story when it came through. It was supported by the captured divisional orders of the German Army in France, and I have an impression it was also backed up by the Foreign Office on the strength of extracts from the German Press. We did not know that it had been invented by anybody, and had we known there was the slightest doubt about the truth of the story, it would not have been used in any way by us.

A New York correspondent describes how he rang General Charteris up, and inquired the truth of the report and suggested that, if untrue, he should take it up with the *New York Times.*

On this he protested vigorously that he could not think of challenging the report, as the mistakes were only of minor importance.

"Daily News," November 5, 1925.

There was a *Times* article on the same subject quoting the *New York Times'* assertion of the truth of their version of the speech.

This paper makes the significant observation that in the course of his denial he offered no comment on his reported admission that he avoided telling the truth when questioned about the matter in the House of Commons, or on his own description of a scheme to support the Corpse Factory story by "planting" a forged diary in the clothing of a dead German prisoner—a proposal which he only abandoned lest the deception might be discovered.

Brigadier-General Charteris, who returned from America at the week-end, visited the War Office yesterday and had an interview with the Secretary of State for War (Sir Laming Worthington-Evans) concerning the reports of his speech on war propaganda in New York. It is understood that the War Office now regard the incident as closed and that no further inquiry is likely to be held.

General Charteris left for Scotland later in the day, and on arrival in Glasgow issued the following statement :

"On arrival in Scotland I was surprised to find that, in spite of the repudiation issued by me at New York through Reuter's agency, some public interest was still excited in the entirely incorrect report of my remarks at a private dinner in New York. I feel it necessary therefore to give again a categorical denial to the statement attributed to me. Certain suggestions and speculations as regards the origins of the *Kadaver* story, which have already been published in *These Eventful Years* (British Encyclopædia Press) and elsewhere, which I repeated, are, doubtless unintentionally, but nevertheless unfortunately, turned into definite statements of fact and attributed to me.

"Lest there should still be any doubt, let me say that I neither invented the *Kadaver* story nor did I alter the captions in any photographs, nor did I use faked material for propaganda purposes. The allegations that I did so are not only incorrect but absurd, as propaganda was in no way under G.H.Q. France, where I had charge of the Intelligence Services. I should be as interested as the general public to know what was the true origin of the *Kadaver* story. G.H.Q. France only came in when a fictitious diary supporting the *Kadaver* story was submitted. When this diary was discovered to be fictitious, it was at once rejected.

"I have seen the Secretary of State this morning and have explained the whole circumstances to him, and have his authority to say that he is perfectly satisfied."

"The Times," November 4, 1925.

LIEUT.-COMMANDER KENWORTHY asked the Secretary of State for War if, in view of the feeling aroused in Germany by the recrudescence of the rumours of the so-called corpse conversion factory behind the German lines in the late war, he can give any information as to the source of the original rumour and the extent to which it was accepted by the War Office at the time.

SIR L. WORTHINGTON-EVANS : At this distance of time I do not think that the source of the rumour can be traced with any certainty. The statement that the Germans had set up a factory for the conversion of dead bodies first appeared on April 10, 1917, in the *Lokalanzeiger*, published in Berlin, and in *l'Indépendance Belge* and *La Belgique*, two Belgian newspapers published in France and Holland. The statements were reproduced in the Press here, with the comment that it was the first German admission concerning the way in which the Germans used their dead bodies.

Questions were asked in the House of Commons on April 30, 1917, and the Under-Secretary of State for Foreign Affairs replied on behalf of the Government that he had then no information beyond that contained in the extract from the German Press. But shortly afterwards a German Army Order containing instructions for the delivery of dead bodies to the establishments described in the *Lokalanzeiger* was captured in France and forwarded to the

War Office, who, after careful consideration, permitted it to be published.

The terms of this order were such that, taken in conjunction with the articles in the *Lokalanzeiger* and in the two Belgian papers and the previously existing rumours, it appeared to the War Office to afford corroborative evidence of the story. Evidence that the word *Kadaver* was used to mean human bodies, and not only carcasses of animals, was found in German dictionaries and anatomical and other works, and the German assertion that the story was disposed of by reference to the meaning of the word *Kadaver* was not accepted. On the information before them at the time, the War Office appear to have seen no reason to disbelieve the truth of the story.

LIEUT.-COMMANDER KENWORTHY : I am much obliged to the Right Hon. Gentleman for his very full answer. Does he not think it desirable now that the War Office should finally disavow the story and their present belief in it ?

SIR L. WORTHINGTON-EVANS : I cannot believe any public interest is served by further questions on this story. I have given the House the fullest information in my possession in the hope that the Hon. Members will be satisfied with what I have said. (HON. MEMBERS : Hear, hear.)

LIEUT.-COMMANDER KENWORTHY : Does not the Right Hon. Gentleman think it desirable, even now, to finally admit the inaccuracy of the original story, in view of Locarno and other things ?

SIR L. WORTHINGTON-EVANS : It is not a question of whether it was accurate or inaccurate. What I was concerned with was the information upon which the War Office acted at the time. Of course, the fact that there has been no corroboration since necessarily alters the complexion of the case, but I was dealing with the information in the possession of the authorities at the time.

House of Commons, November 24, 1925.

This was a continued attempt to avoid making a complete denial, and it was left to Sir Austen Chamberlain to nail the lie finally to the counter. In reply to

Mr. Arthur Henderson on December 2, 1925, asking if he had any statement to make as to the *Kadaver* story, he said :

> Yes, sir ; my Right Hon. Friend the Secretary of State for War told the House last week how the story reached His Majesty's Government in 1917. The Chancellor of the German Reich has authorized me to say, on the authority of the German Government, that there was never any foundation for it. I need scarcely add that on behalf of His Majesty's Government I accept this denial, and I trust that this false report will not again be revived.

The painful impression made by this episode and similar propaganda efforts in America is well illustrated by an editorial in *Times-Dispatch*, of Richmond, U.S.A., on December 6, 1925.

> Not the least of the horrors of modern warfare is the propaganda bureau, which is an important item in the military establishment of every nation. Neither is it the least of the many encouraging signs which each year add to the probability of eventual peace on earth. The famous *Kadaver* story, which aroused hatred against the German to the boiling-point in this and other Allied nations during the war, has been denounced as a lie in the British House of Commons. Months ago the world learned the details of how this lie was planned and broadcasted by the efficient officer in the British Intelligence Service. Now we are told that, imbued with the spirit of the Locarno pact, Sir Austen Chamberlain rose in the House, said that the German Chancellor had denied the truth of the story, and that the denial had been accepted by the British Government.
>
> A few years ago the story of how the Kaiser was reducing human corpses to fat aroused the citizens of this and other enlightened nations to a fury of hatred. Normally sane men doubled their fists and rushed off to the nearest recruiting sergeant. Now they are being told, in effect, that they were dupes and fools ; that their own officers deliberately goaded them to the desired boiling-point, using an infamous

lie to arouse them, just as a grown bully whispers to one little boy that another little boy said he could lick him.

The encouraging sign found in this revolting admission of how modern war is waged is the natural inference that the modern man is not over-eager to throw himself at his brother's throat at the simple word of command. His passions must be played upon, so the propaganda bureau has taken its place as one of the chief weapons.

In the next war, the propaganda must be more subtle and clever than the best the World War produced. These frank admissions of wholesale lying on the part of trusted Governments in the last war will not soon be forgotten.

H

XVIII

THE BISHOP OF ZANZIBAR'S LETTER

THERE are two things which cannot be permitted during war. Firstly, favourable comment on the enemy—instances of this have been given in the Introduction. Secondly, criticism of the country to which you belong cannot be publicly expressed. Suppression of opinion of this kind is all very well, but the deliberate distortion of it is a peculiarly malicious form of falsehood.

The late Dr. Weston, Bishop of Zanzibar, a great champion of the African natives, wrote an open letter to General Smuts, in which he said :

> It is political madness at this time of day to try and subject a weaker people to serfdom, or to slavery. . . . It is moral madness. . . . Thirdly, it is so definitely an anti-Christian policy that no one who adopts it can any longer justify the Gospel of Christ to the African peoples. . . .

In a pamphlet quoted in the *Church Times*, October 8, 1920, the Bishop of Zanzibar wrote :

> When I wrote my open letter to General Smuts I called it " Great Britain's Scrap of Paper : Will She Honour It ? " I was alluding to her promise of justice to the weaker peoples. The Imperial Government took my letter, cut out some inconvenient passages, and published it under the title, " The Black Slaves of Prussia." I suggest that East Africans have now become the " Black Serfs of Great Britain."

In the *Life of the Bishop of Zanzibar*, published in

1926, the letter appears in its garbled form as the Bishop's opinion of the German treatment of their " black slaves."

This is a good instance of a quite deliberate perversion by the Government and also an instance of how difficult it is for the truth, even when published, to overtake a lie and to reach the people most concerned.

XIX

THE GERMAN U-BOAT OUTRAGE

A MONSTROUS story of fiendish cruelty on the part of a German U-boat commander was circulated in the Press in July 1918. It is an instance of how people in positions of semi-official authority were either ready deliberately to invent or to elaborate some vague rumour and give it the stamp of authentic information.

It appeared in more or less the same form in all the newspapers :

Staff-Paymaster Collingwood Hughes, R.N.V.R., of the Naval Intelligence Division of the Admiralty, lecturing yesterday at the Royal Club, St. James's Square, said that one of our patrol boats in the Atlantic found a derelict U-boat. After rescuing the crew our commander inquired of the Hun captain if all were safely aboard, as it was intended to blow up the U-boat.

"Yes," came the reply, "they are here. Call the roll." Every German answered. The British commander was about to push off before dropping a depth charge, when tapping was heard.

"Are you quite sure there is no one on board your boat ? " he repeated.

"Yes," declared the Hun captain.

But the tapping continued, and the British officer ordered a search of the U-boat. There were found in it, tied up as prisoners, four British seamen. The rescued Germans were going to allow their prisoners to be drowned.

" Daily Mail," July 12, 1918.

The story was repeated by Commander Sir Edward Nicholl at a public meeting at Colston Hall, in Bristol, at which the Parliamentary Secretary to the Admiralty was present.

COLONEL WEDGWOOD asked the First Lord of the Admiralty whether one of our patrol boats recently rescued the crew of a derelict U-boat, the captain of which deliberately left on board four British seamen, who would have been drowned if they had not been heard knocking and been rescued; and if this is so, what steps have been taken to deal with the captain of the U-boat.

THE PARLIAMENTARY SECRETARY TO THE ADMIRALTY (Dr. Macnamara) : The Admiralty have officially stated in the public Press that they have no knowledge of this reported incident and that the statement was made without their authority.

COLONEL WEDGWOOD : Are we to understand that this statement is absolutely without any basis of fact and is, in fact, a lie ?

DR. MACNAMARA : We have stated that we have no information in confirmation of the statement which was made.

House of Commons, July 15, 1918.

In reply to subsequent questions Dr. Macnamara stated he was getting into communication with the officer responsible for the statement.

COLONEL WEDGWOOD asked the First Lord of the Admiralty whether the story about the derelict U-boat has yet been reported on, and, if so, what conclusion has been come to ; and whether the story was first told by a naval officer at a meeting at the Colston Hall about five weeks ago, at which the Parliamentary Secretary himself was present.

DR. MACNAMARA : We have endeavoured to trace this story to its origin. Fleet-Paymaster Collingwood Hughes appears to have heard it from more than one source. He should certainly have taken the opportunity afforded him in his official position to verify it. In our opinion the story is without foundation. As regards the second part of the question, Commander Sir Edward Nicholl, Royal Naval Reserve, certainly told the story in the course of a speech at a meeting at Bristol, at which I was present. I learn from him that he was present at an earlier meeting addressed by Mr. Collingwood Hughes in South Wales and heard the story recited by him on that occasion.

House of Commons, July 23, 1918.

But, of course, in this, as in other cases, for one person who noticed the denial there were a thousand who only heard the lie.

XX

CONSTANTINOPLE

THE evasions and concealments necessitated by the existence of the Secret Treaties cover too large a ground to be dealt with here. Evasion is a more insidious form of falsehood than the deliberate lie. One point, however, which was of considerable interest to the people of Great Britain may serve as an illustration. It concerned the fate of Constantinople.

Asked in the House of Commons on May 30, 1916, whether Professor Miliukoff's statement in the Duma was correct, that "our supreme aim in this war is to get possession of Constantinople, which must belong to Russia entirely and without reserve," Sir Edward Grey replied that "it is not necessary or desirable to make official comments on unofficial statements," and being further pressed, added, "The Honourable Member is asking for a statement which I do not think it desirable to make."

From the point of view of the Government, the Foreign Secretary was quite right to evade the question. In the first place we had not taken Constantinople, and in the second place it must have appeared doubtful to the Government whether the British soldiers and sailors would be enthusiastic in sacrificing their lives in order to give Constantinople to Russia, the strains of the old jingo song of 1878 not having quite died away :

We've fought the Bear before, we can fight the Bear again,
But the Russians shall not have Constantinople.

But on March 7, 1915, a year before Sir E. Grey gave this answer in Parliament, M. Sazonov had telegraphed to the Russian Ambassador in London :

Will you please express to Grey the profound gratitude of the Imperial Government for the complete and final assent of Great Britain to the solution of the question of the Straits and Constantinople in accordance with Russian desires.

On December 2, 1916, M. Trepoff declared in the Duma :

An agreement, which we concluded in 1915 with Great Britain and France and to which Italy has adhered, established in the most definite fashion the right of Russia to the Straits and Constantinople. . . . I repeat that absolute agreement on this point is firmly established among the Allies.

On January 5, 1918 (National War Aims Pamphlet No. 33), the Prime Minister declared that we were not fighting " to deprive Turkey of its capital." He could say this because the Russian Revolution had taken place.

By subterfuges and evasions the British Government were anxious to screen the truth from the country, because they knew how unpopular it would be.

XXI

THE " LUSITANIA "

THE sinking of the *Lusitania* was a hideous tragedy and one of the most terrible examples of the barbarity of modern warfare, but, from the point of view of suffering and loss of life, was not to be compared with many other episodes in the war. The very crucial political significance of the catastrophe, however, gave it special propaganda value in inflaming popular indignation, specially in America. Here obviously was the necessary lever at last to bring America into the war. That Germany should not have recognized that this would be the result of such action on her part was one of the many illustrations of her total inability to grasp the psychology of other peoples.

From the point of view of propaganda it was necessary to show that the Germans had blown up a defenceless passenger ship flying the American flag and bearing only civilian passengers and an ordinary cargo. This was represented as a breach of international law and an act of piracy. The unsuccessful attempt to suppress certain facts which emerged leads naturally to the conclusion that other attempts were successful. No inquiry, such as the Mersey inquiry, conducted in war-time with regard to the action of the enemy, can in such circumstances be regarded as conclusive.

The whole truth with regard to the sinking of the *Lusitania* will probably never be cleared up. Four points may be considered here :

(*a*) Whether she was armed.

(*b*) Whether she was carrying Canadian troops.

(*c*) Whether she had munitions on board.

(*d*) Whether a medal was issued in Germany to commemorate the sinking of the *Lusitania*.

(*a*) On this point there was a conflict of evidence. The *Lusitania* was registered as an auxiliary cruiser. The Germans declared she was carrying concealed guns. This was categorically denied by the captain in the inquiry. " She had no weapons of offence or defence and no masked guns." Lord Mersey therefore found this charge to be untrue.

(*b*) The same may be said about the charge made by the Germans that she was transporting Canadian troops.

(*c*) These two denials would be readily acceptable, were it not for the fact that at first a denial and then a suppression of the fact that she was carrying munitions was attempted.

It is equally untrue that the *Lusitania* was carrying ammunition on its final voyage.

" *Daily Express,*" May 11, 1915.

In America there was a threat to expel Senator La Follette from the Senate because he had stated that the *Lusitania* carried munitions. But Mr. Dudley Field Malone, collector at the port of New York, confirmed this charge as true.

D. F. Malone revealed that the *Lusitania* carried large quantities of ammunition consigned to the British Government, including 4,200 cases of Springfield cartridges. The Wilson administration refused to permit the publication of the fact. One of the principal charges upon which the attempt to expel R. M. La Follette from the Senate was based was that he had falsely declared that the *Lusitania* carried ammunition, and the prosecution of the Senator was dropped when Mr. Malone offered to testify on his behalf.

" The Nation " (New York), November 20, 1920.

It was eventually admitted that the *Lusitania* carried 5,400 cases of ammunition. The captain at the inquest at Kinsale said : " There was a second report, but that might possibly have been an internal explosion." The foreman of the Queenstown jury protested that all the victims were not drowned. " I have seen many of the bodies, and the people were killed ; they were blown to pieces."

The ship sank in eighteen minutes, which accounted for the loss of so many lives. The Germans, in their reply to the American note, referred to this point and stated :

It is impossible to decide, for instance, the question whether the necessary opportunity was given to the passengers and crew to escape, until it has been determined whether or not the *Lusitania* provided bulkheads and boats as ordered by the *Titanic* Conference for corresponding emergencies in peace-time, and whether or not ammunition or explosives carried in defiance of the American laws accelerated the sinking of the ship, which might otherwise have been expected either to get out the boats safely or reach the coast.

Included in her cargo was a small consignment of rifle ammunition and shrapnel shells weighing about 173 tons. Warnings that the vessel would be sunk, afterwards traced to the German Government, were circulated in New York before she sailed.

" The World Crisis," by the Right Hon. Winston Churchill, M.P.

(*d*) The event having been condemned as a barbarous act of piracy, it became necessary to show that the Germans gloried in it.

The first rumour was that a special medal had been bestowed on the crew of the U-boat which sunk the *Lusitania* as a reward for gallantry. This was dropped when the medal turned out to be a commemoration medal, not a decoration.

It was then stated that the German Government had had a medal struck in commemoration of the event, but after the armistice had it withdrawn from circulation. In 1919 it was found in a shop in Berlin. In 1920 a traveller in Berlin, Frankfurt, and other parts of Germany could find no one who had ever heard of it or seen it, whereas in England the medals were well known and very easily obtained. It turned out that the medal was originally designed in Munich by a man of the name of Goetz and represents the *Lusitania* as carrying arms. Goetz may be described as a cartoonist in metal; his work was not official, and his *Lusitania* medal had a very limited circulation. Few Germans appear to have heard of its existence. The large number of casts of the medal, which gave the impression here that they must be as common as pence in Germany, was explained by Lord Newton, who was in charge of propaganda at the Foreign Office in 1916.

I asked a West End store if they could undertake the reproduction of it for propaganda purposes. They agreed to do so, and the medals were sold all over the world in neutral countries, especially in America and South America. After some initial difficulty a great success was achieved. I believe it to have been one of the best pieces of propaganda.
        " Evening Standard," November 1, 1926.

The Honorary Secretary of the *Lusitania* Medal Committee stated that 250,000 of the medals were sold, and the proceeds were given to the Red Cross and St. Dunstan's. Each medal was enclosed in a box on

which it was stated that the medals were replicas of
the medal distributed in Germany " to commemorate
the sinking of the *Lusitania*." But many of them in
England could be purchased without any box.

In addition to the medal, leaflets were circulated with
pictures of the medal. In one case in Sweden a sentence
was printed from the *Kölnische Völkszeitung*: " We
regard with joyous pride this newest exploit of our
fleet." This sentence had been torn from its context,
and had been originally used in quite another connection.

It therefore became clear that :

(1) No medal was given to the crew of the German
     U-boat.
(2) No medal was struck in commemoration of the
     event by the German Government.
(3) The German Government could not have with-
     drawn a medal it never issued.
(4) A metal-worker in Munich designed the medal,
     which was always rare in Germany.
(5) The large number of medals in circulation was
     due to the reproduction of Goetz's medal in
     Great Britain.

The propaganda value of the medal was great, as
Lord Newton admitted. The impression it created was
absolutely and intentionally false.

XXII

REPORT OF A BROKEN-UP MEETING

THERE were official eavesdroppers, telephone-tappers, letter-openers, etc., by the score. We are not concerned with their activities here. But it may be imagined what a large crop of spy stories and "authentic" tales they originated. An amusing instance may be given of an official who was sent to attend and report on a meeting of the Union of Democratic Control, held at the Memorial Hall in November 1915. Major R. M. Mackay (Argyll and Sutherland Highlanders) was Assistant Provost-Marshal, and sent in a report, most of which was read out in the House of Commons by Mr. Tennant, Under-Secretary at the War Office, on December 7th. Attention was called to the meeting, because it was broken up by soldiers who had obtained forged tickets. The Assistant Provost-Marshal's report was so fantastic that it almost appeared as if he could not have been at the meeting at all. But, of course, the evidence of such a high-placed official was accepted as conclusive. He accused Mr. Ramsay MacDonald of having provoked the soldiers by sending a message to have some of them ejected. There was not a shred of truth in this. He reported that someone "whose name I could not ascertain" had used provocative language. He described stewardesses "who not only appeared to be Teutonic but could be classified as such from their accents," whose remarks he overheard. Needless to say, there was no Teuton or anyone with a Teutonic accent in the building.

On a subsequent occasion, when Mr. Tennant attempted to explain away parts of the report he had read out, the following comment appeared in the *Westminster Gazette* :

Mr. Tennant explained that his answer, with its references to stewardesses with " Teutonic accents " and its attribution to Mr. Ramsay MacDonald of words which were never used, was read hurriedly from a report made to him. Ministers are compelled to depend on such reports, but the language ought to be severely edited before it comes before the House of Commons. If that precaution is neglected, Ministers lay up for themselves an amount of irritation and resentment which is wholly unnecessary.

In 1917 the reliable Provost-Marshal was accused of wrongful arrest. In May 1918 he was charged with " lending " soldiers as gardeners, etc., to his personal friends, misuse of public money, etc. Some of the many charges against him were dismissed, but later in the same year it was announced that he was " dismissed the service by sentence of General Court Martial " (*London Gazette Supplement, August* 12, 1918).

It came out in evidence *that he had been deaf for years.*

XXIII

ATROCITY STORIES

WAR is, in itself, an atrocity. Cruelty and suffering are inherent in it. Deeds of violence and barbarity occur, as everyone knows. Mankind is goaded by authority to indulge every elemental animal passion. But the exaggeration and invention of atrocities soon becomes the main staple of propaganda. Stories of German " frightfulness " in Belgium were circulated in such numbers as to give ample proof of the abominable cruelty of the German Army and so to infuriate popular opinion against them. A Belgian commission was appointed, and subsequently a commission, under the chairmanship of Lord Bryce, who was chosen in order that opinion in America, where he had been a very popular ambassador, might be impressed. Affidavits of single witnesses were accepted as conclusive proof.

At best, human testimony is unreliable, even in ordinary occurrences of no consequence, but where bias, sentiment, passion, and so-called patriotism disturb the emotions, a personal affirmation becomes of no value whatsoever.

To cover the whole ground on atrocity stories would be impossible. They were circulated in leaflets, pamphlets, letters, and speeches day after day. Prominent people of repute, who would have shrunk from condemning their bitterest personal enemy on the evidence, or rather lack of evidence, they had before them, did not hesitate to lead the way in charging a whole nation with every conceivable brutality and unnatural crime. *The*

Times issued " Marching Songs," written by a prominent
Eton master, in which such lines as these occurred :

> He shot the wives and children,
> The wives and little children ;
> He shot the wives and children,
> And laughed to see them die.

One or two instances of the proved falsity of statements made by people under the stress of excitement
and indignation may be given.

It was reported that some thirty to thirty-five German
soldiers entered the house of David Tordens, a carter,
in Sempst ; they bound him, and then five or six of
them assaulted and ravished in his presence his thirteen-
year-old daughter, and afterwards fixed her on bayonets.
After this horrible deed, they bayoneted his nine-year-old
boy and then shot his wife. His life was saved through
the timely arrival of Belgian soldiers. It was further
asserted that all the girls in Sempst were assaulted and
ravished by the Germans.

The secretary of the commune, Paul van Boeckpourt,
the mayor, Peter van Asbroeck, and his son Louis van
Asbroeck, in a sworn statement made on April 4, 1915,
at Sempst, declared that the name given to the carter,
David Tordens, was quite unknown to them ; that
such a person did not live in Sempst before the war and
was quite unknown in the commune ; that during the
war no woman or child under fourteen was killed in
Sempst, and if such an occurrence had taken place they
would certainly have heard of it.[1]

Another report published was that at Ternath the
Germans met a boy and asked him the way to Thurt.
As the boy did not understand them, they chopped off
both his hands.

[1] Quoted in *Truth*: "A Path to Justice and Reconciliation," by
" Verax."

I

Statement by the Mayor of Ternath, Dr. Poodt, on February 11, 1915 :

" I declare there is not a word of truth in it. I have been in Ternath since the beginning of the war, and it is impossible that such an occurrence should not have been reported to me ; it is a pure invention."

After the publication of the various reports, five American war correspondents issued the following declaration :

To let the truth be known, we unanimously declare the stories of German cruelties, from what we have been able to observe, were untrue. After having been with the German Army for two weeks, and having accompanied the troops for over one hundred miles, we are not able to report one single case of undeserved punishment or measure of retribution. We are neither able to confirm any rumours as regards maltreatment of prisoners and non-combatants. Having been with the German troops through Landen, Brussels, Nivelles, Buissière, Haute-Wiherie, Merbes-le-Château, Sorle-sur-Sambre, Beaumont, we have not the slightest basis for making up a case of excess. We found numerous rumours after investigation to be without foundation. German soldiers paid everywhere for what they bought, and respected private property and civil rights. We found Belgian women and children after the battle of Buissière to feel absolutely safe. A citizen was shot in Merbes-le-Château, but nobody could prove his innocence. Refugees, who told about cruelties and brutalities, could bring absolutely no proof. The discipline of the German soldiers is excellent ; no drunkenness. The Burgomaster of Sorle-sur-Sambre voluntarily disclaimed all rumours of cruelties in that district. For the truth of the above we pledge our word of honour as journalists.

> (*Signed*) Roger Lewis, Associated Press ; Irwin Cobb, *Saturday Evening Post, Philadelphia Public Ledger*, Philadelphia ; Harry Hansen, *Chicago Daily News*, Chicago ; James O'Donnell Bennett, *Chicago Tribune* ; John T. McCutcheon, *Chicago Tribune*, Chicago.

In the issue of the *New York World* of January 28, 1915, appeared the following dispatch :

Washington, January 27th.—Of the thousands of Belgian refugees who are now in England, not one has been subjected to atrocities by German soldiers. This, in effect, is the substance of a report received at the State Department. The report states that the British Government had investigated thousands of reports to the effect that German soldiers had perpetrated outrages on fleeing Belgians. During the early period of the war columns of British newspapers were filled with the accusation. Agents of the British Government, according to the report of the American Embassy in London, carefully investigated all these charges ; they interviewed the alleged victims and sifted all the evidence. As a result of the investigation, the British Foreign Office notified the American Embassy that the charges appeared to be based upon hysteria and natural prejudice. The report added that many of the Belgians had suffered hardships, but they should be charged up against the exigence of war rather than to brutality of the individual German soldiers.

The following passage occurs in a review by the *New York Times Literary Supplement* of March 19, 1918, of " Brave Belgians," by Baron C. Buttin, to which Baron de Brocqueville, the Belgian Minister of War, contributed a preface commending its truth and fairness :

The work gives eye-witness accounts of the first three months of the invasion of Belgium, and is made up of reports told by various people who did their share in that extraordinary resistance—colonels, majors, and army chaplains, lieutenants, etc. There is scarcely a hint of that " bugbear," German atrocities, or the nameless or needless horrors described in the report of the Bryce Commission.

An amazing instance of the way atrocity lies may still remain fixed in some people's minds, and how an attempt may be made to propagate them even now, is afforded by a letter which appeared as recently as April 12, 1927, in the *Evening Star*, Dunedin, New Zealand. The writer, Mr. Gordon Catto, answering another correspondent on the subject of atrocities, wrote :

My wife, who in 1914–15 was a nurse in the Ramsgate General Hospital, England, actually nursed Belgian women and children refugees who were the victims of Hun rapacity and fiendishness, the women having had their breasts cut off and the children with their hands hacked off at the wrists.

Here was almost first-hand evidence noting both time and place. An inquiry was accordingly addressed by a lady investigator to the Secretary of the Ramsgate General Hospital, and the following reply was received :

Ramsgate General Hospital, 4, Cannon Road, Ramsgate,

11. 6. 27.

DEAR MADAM,
I am at a loss to know how the information about atrocities to women and children, committed by the German soldiers, could have originated in respect to Ramsgate, as there were no such cases received.
Yours faithfully,
(*Signed*) SYDNEY W. SMITH.

An instance of a man being genuinely misled by the information given him, not having any desire himself to propagate lies, can be given in the case of a Baptist minister of Sheffield, who preached on atrocities. On February 28, 1915, preaching in Wash Lane Baptist Chapel, Letchford, Warrington, he told the congregation that there was a Belgian girl in Sheffield, about twelve years old, who had had her nose cut off and her stomach ripped open by the Germans, but she was still living and getting better.

On inquiry being made as to whether he had made this statement, he replied :

I have written to our Belgian Consul here for the name and address of the girl whose case I quoted at Letchford. If all I hear is true, it is far worse than I stated.

I am also asking for another similar instance, which I shall be glad to transmit to you if, and as soon as, I can secure the facts.

The Belgian Consul, in a letter of March 11th, wrote :

Although I have heard of a number of cases of Belgian girls being maltreated in one way and another, I have on investigation not found a particle of truth in one of them, and I know of no girl in Sheffield who has had her nose cut off and her stomach ripped open.

I have also investigated cases in other towns, but have not yet succeeded in getting hold of any tangible confirmation.

The minister accordingly informed his correspondent :

I am writing a letter to my old church at Letchford to be read on Sunday next, contradicting the story which I told on what seemed to be unimpeachable authority. I am glad I did not give the whole alleged facts as they were given to me.

With many thanks for your note and inquiry.

It is to be feared, however, that his first congregation, satisfied with pulpit confirmation of the story, circulated it beyond the reach of the subsequent denial.

Atrocity stories from the foreign Press could scarcely be collected in a library. A glance through any foreign newspaper will show that hardly a page in hardly an issue is free from them. In Eastern Europe they were particularly horrible. They were the almost conventional form of journalistic expression on all sides. The brutalization of the European mind was very thoroughly carried out. But moral indignation and even physical nausea were checked by the surfeit of horrors and the blatant exaggerations. There can be no more discreditable period in the history of journalism than the four years of the Great War.

A neutral paper (*Nieuwe Courant*), published at The Hague, summed up the effect of propaganda on January 17, 1916 :

> . . . The paper war-propaganda is a poison, which outsiders can only stand in very small doses. If the belligerents continue to administer it the effect will be the opposite to that expected. So it goes with the stream of literature on the Cavell case, and the varied forms in which the *Baralong* poison is presented to us. We leave it with a certain disgust, after tasting it, and are only annoyed at the bitter after-taste—the promised reprisals. . . .

XXIV

FAKED PHOTOGRAPHS

To the uninitiated there is something substantially reliable in a picture obviously taken from a photograph. Nothing would seem to be more authentic than a snapshot. It does not occur to anyone to question a photograph, and faked pictures therefore have special value, as they get a much better start than any mere statement, which may be criticized or denied. Only a long time after, if ever, can their falsity be detected. The faking of photographs must have amounted almost to an industry during the war. All countries were concerned, but the French were the most expert. Some of the originals have been collected and reproduced.[1]

Descriptions of a few of them may be given here :

In *Das Echo*, October 29, 1914, there was a photograph of the German troops marching along a country road in Belgium.

This was reproduced by *Le Journal* on November 26, 1914, under the title :

LES ALLEMANDS EN RETRAITE.

Cette photographie fournit une vision saississante de ce que fut la retraite de l'armée du général von Hindenburg après la bataille de la Vistule.

A photograph taken by Karl Delius, of Berlin, showed the delivery of mail-bags in front of the Field Post Office in Kavevara.

[1] *How the World Madness was Engineered*, by Ferdinand Avenarius.

This was reproduced in the *Daily Mirror* of December 3, 1915, with the title :

MADE TO WASH THE HUNS' DIRTY LINEN.

The blond beasts are sweating the Serbians, who are made to do the washing for the invaders. Like most customers who do not settle their bills, they are full of grumbles and complaints. Here a pile has just arrived from the wash.

Several photographs were taken during the pogrom in Russia in 1905; some of these were circulated by Jews in America. One of these photographs represented a row of corpses with a crowd round them, and was reproduced in *Le Miroir*, November 14, 1915, with the title :

LES CRIMES DES HORDES ALLEMANDES EN POLOGNE.

Several others of these were similarly reproduced in newspapers. The *Critica*, a newspaper in the Argentine, exposed German atrocities by this means.

A photograph was taken in Berlin of a crowd before the royal palace on July 13, 1914 (before the outbreak of war). This was reproduced in *Le Monde Illustré*, August 21, 1915, with the heading :

ENTHOUSIASME ET JOIE DE BARBARES,

with an explanation that it was a demonstration to celebrate the sinking of the *Lusitania*.

A photograph which appeared in the Berlin *Tag*, on August 13, 1914, represented a long queue of men with basins. Under it was written :

How we treat interned Russian and French ; lining up the interned before the distribution of food.

This was reproduced in the *Daily News* on April 2, 1915, with the title :

GERMAN WORKERS FEEL THE PINCH.

The above crowd lining up for rations is a familiar sight in Germany.   It reveals one aspect of our naval power.

A photograph of German officers inspecting munition cases was reproduced by *War Illustrated*, January 30, 1915, as " German officers pillaging chests in a French château."

A photograph of a German soldier bending over a fallen German comrade was reproduced in *War Illustrated*, April 17, 1915, with the title :

Definite proof of the Hun's abuse of the rules of war. German ghoul actually caught in the act of robbing a Russian.

In the *Berlin Lokalanzeiger* of June 9, 1914, a photograph was published of three cavalry officers who had won cups and other trophies, which they are holding, at the Army steeplechase in the Grunewald.

This was first reproduced in *Wes Mir*, a Russian newspaper, with the title " The German Looters in Warsaw," and also, on August 8, 1915, by the *Daily Mirror* with the title :

THREE GERMAN CAVALRYMEN LOADED WITH GOLD AND SILVER LOOT.

Faked photographs were, of course, sent in great numbers to neutral countries.

A German photograph of the town of Schwirwindt, after the Russian occupation, was reproduced in *Illustreret Familieblad* (Denmark) as, " A French City after a German Bombardment."

A photograph from *Das Leben in Bild*, in 1917, of three young German soldiers laughing, was entitled :

Home again. Three sturdy young Germans who succeeded in escaping from French imprisonment.

This came out in a Danish family paper on May 2, 1917, as :

Escaped from drumfire hell. Three German soldiers apparently very happy to have become French prisoners of war.

The citadel at Brest-Litovsk was fired by the retreating Russians, and a photograph appeared in *Zeitbilder*, September 5, 1915, showing Germans carrying out the corn in sacks.

This was reproduced in the *Graphic*, September 18, 1915, as, " German soldiers plundering a factory at Brest-Litovsk, which was fired by the retreating Russians."

Illustrated War News, December 29, 1915, gave a photograph of war trophies. A sergeant is holding up a sort of cat-o'-nine-tails whip.

WHAT WAS IT USED FOR ? A GERMAN WHIP AMONG A COLLECTION OF WAR TROPHIES.

These war trophies captured from the Germans in Flanders have been presented to the Irish Rifles by a sergeant. The presence of the whip is of curious significance.

The " whip," as a matter of fact, was an ordinary German carpet-beater.

A Russian film represented German nurses in the garb of religious sisters stabbing the wounded on the battlefield.

A picture, not a photograph, which had a great

circulation, was called *Chemin de la gloire* (the Road of Glory) in the *Choses Vues* (Things Seen) series.

In the background is a cathedral in flames, a long road is strewn with bottles, and in the foreground is the body of a little boy impaled to the ground by a bayonet.

But if pictures and caricatures were to be described, there would be no end of it. Undoubtedly the cartoonist had a great influence in all countries, especially Raemakers and *Punch*. The unfortunate neutral countries were bombarded with them from both sides.

A remarkable series of photographs was taken by a Mr. F. J. Mortimer, Fellow of the Royal Photographic Society, and published in 1912. They were widely reproduced in illustrated periodicals. Among them was a photograph of the *Arden Craig* sinking off the Scilly Isles in January 1911. On March 31, 1917, a popular illustrated weekly devoted a page to " Camera Records of Prussian Piracy," and this particular photograph was reproduced in a succession of pictures to illustrate " a windjammer torpedoed off the English coast by the criminally indiscriminate U-boat pirates."

Mr. Mortimer's photographs of British ships were also reproduced in Germany under the heading of " Scenes from the German Navy."

On September 28, 1916, the *Daily Sketch* gave a photograph of a crowd of German prisoners under the heading " Still They Come ! " " Between 3,000 and 4,000 prisoners have been taken in the past forty-eight hours." (Official.)

On October 10, 1918, the *Daily Mirror* reproduced precisely the same photograph, under which was printed : " Just a very small portion of the Allies' unique collection of Hun war prisoners of the 1918 season."

XXV

THE DOCTORING OF OFFICIAL PAPERS

PRESS lies and private lies may in certain circumstances carry much weight. At the same time there are often sections of the public who are less credulous, and therefore more suspicious. But when printed documents appear with an official imprimatur—in this country the royal arms and the superscription "Presented to Parliament by command of His Majesty," or "Printed by order of the House of Commons"—everyone believes that in these papers, at any rate, they have got the whole truth and nothing but the truth. Only a minority, perhaps, study them, but this minority writes and furnishes the Press with indisputably authentic information from "command papers." The blue books, yellow books, white books, orange books, etc., become the basis of all propaganda.

It comes as a shock therefore to those who patriotically accept their Government's story to find that instances of *suppressio veri* abound in the form of passages carefully and intentionally suppressed from published official documents.

This practice, of course, did not originate during the Great War. It is an old diplomatic tradition, justified conceivably in cases where the concealment of injudicious language on the part of a foreign statesman may prevent the inflammation of public opinion, but carried to unjustifiable lengths when a concealment or distortion of the facts of the case is aimed at.

Sir Edward Grey's speech on August 3rd was a very meagre and incomplete recital of events given to a House which had been deliberately kept ignorant for years. But it was well framed to have the desired effect. Amongst the omissions was the German Ambassador's proposal of August 1st, in which he suggested that Germany might be willing to guarantee not only Belgian neutrality but also the integrity of France and that of her colonies, and the Foreign Secretary further omitted to mention that in this interview he had definitely refused to formulate any conditions on which the neutrality of the country might be guaranteed, though the Ambassador requested him to do so. But by far the most serious omission was his failure to read to the House the last sentence in his letter to M. Cambon, a sentence of vital importance. The sentence ran :

If these measures involved action, the plans of the General Staff would at once be taken into consideration, and the Government would then decide what effect should be given to them.

This omission is far from being satisfactorily explained in *Twenty-Five Years* by the casual statement, " Perhaps I thought the last sentence unimportant."

The speeches of Ministers in the other European Governments concerned at the time were, of course, all patriotically distorted, and any information with regard to facts which might qualify or mitigate the iniquity of the opposite party was carefully suppressed.

The omission of dispatches or suppressions of passages in the official books of all the Governments are far too numerous even to give as a list.

Some of the British suppressions are now apparent, since the publication by the Foreign Office of further diplomatic documents. Only a couple of examples need be given.

In a telegram of July 24, 1914, from our Ambassador at St. Petersburg, a passage was completely suppressed, in which he indicated the agreement arrived at between France and Russia during the visit of the President, according to which they settled not to tolerate any interference on the part of Austria in the interior affairs of Serbia. In view of what was going on in Serbia, this was highly significant.

A telegram appeared in the White Paper of 1914 from the French Government, dated July 20th, saying that "reservists have been called up by tens of thousands in Germany." But a telegram from the British Ambassador in Berlin of August 1st, saying that no calling up of reserves had yet taken place (404), was suppressed.

Special official reports had to be given the necessary war bias. Here is an instance from one of the Dominions :

A unanimous resolution was adopted on June 29, 1926, by the Council of South-West Africa. This body consider the Blue Book of the South African Union directed against the administration of German South-West Africa merely as an instrument of war, and asked the Government to destroy copies of the book existing among official documents or in the bookshops. In his reply, the Prime Minister of South Africa, General Hertzog, declared that he and his colleagues in the Government could appreciate the causes of the Council's resolution, and that he was prepared to fall in as far as possible with its wishes. In his opinion, the unreliable and unworthy character of this document condemned it to dishonourable burial, together with all kindred publications of the war period.
    Dr. Schnee's complaint re mandated African territories. "The Times," May 16, 1927.

The French Yellow Book was a mass of suppressions,

mutilations, and even falsifications. As a French writer who has carefully examined this whole question writes : [1] " The Government cut out of the Yellow Book everything which concerned the Russian mobilization like a criminal obliterates all traces of his crime." M. Demartial devotes a volume to the various ways in which this official record was tampered with in order to deceive the French people, and he asks : " If the French Government is innocent with regard to the war, why has it falsified the collection of diplomatic documents which expose the origins ? "

There were omissions, too, in the German official White Book, as, for instance, a telegram from the Czar, in which he proposed to submit the Austro-Serbian dispute to arbitration.

A famous case of falsification was the report issued by the Kurt Eisner revolutionary Government at Munich in November 1918 which purported to give the text of a dispatch from the Bavarian Minister at Berlin. As published, this report showed the German Government cynically contemplating the explosion of a world war as the result of Austria's proposed coercive measures against Serbia. The incident gave rise to a libel action. Twelve foreign authorities examined the document, and all of them came to the conclusion that there had been falsification. The French Professor of the Sorbonne, M. Edouard Dujardin, declared : " I am of opinion that the text such as published by the *Bayerische Staatzeitung* is one of the most manifest and most criminal falsifications known to history." The full text showed that the German Government was contemplating not a world war but a localized war between Austria and Serbia.

[1] *L'Évangile du Quai d'Orsay*, by George Demartial.

But whatever may be said about suppressions by other Governments, there is nothing to equal the doctoring and garbling of the Russian Orange Book. The omission not only of passages but of a whole series of important telegrams and dispatches which passed between the Russian Minister for Foreign Affairs, Sazonov, and the Russian Ambassador in Paris, Isvolsky, shows the determination to conceal the real attitude of Russia and France during the critical days, and the insertion of these suppressed documents, which was subsequently made possible, puts a very different complexion on the origins of the outbreak of war than that which was accepted at the time.[1]

Among the suppressions were a telegram stating that "Germany ardently desired the localization of the conflict" (July 24th)—"Counsels of moderation. . . . We have to reject all these at the outset"; telegrams showing the German Ambassador's anxiety for peace; telegrams showing the warlike spirit of France and instructions to the Russians to continue their preparations as quickly as possible (July 30–31). "The French Government have firmly decided upon war and begged me to confirm the hope of the French General Staff that all our efforts will be directed against Germany and that Austria will be treated as a *quantité négligeable.*" In some cases sentences were omitted and in many cases the whole telegram was suppressed.

Statesmen in all countries, whom it would be foolish to describe as dishonourable men, would shrink with disgust from falsifying their own private or business correspondence. Were they to do so, they would be convicted by their own law courts as criminals and

---

[1] The text of the suppressed documents is given in *Duty to Civilization,* by Francis Nielson.

condemned by public opinion. Yet, acting on behalf of their country, with issues at stake of such vast significance, they do not hesitate to lend themselves to a deliberate attempt to mislead their people and the world, and to endeavour to justify their attitude by resorting to the meanest tricks.

XXVI

HYPOCRITICAL INDIGNATION

GAS warfare and submarine warfare offered instances of violent outbursts of indignation on the part of the Press, which events showed were gross hypocrisy. This is an attitude rather than an expression of falsehood.

We must expect the Germans to fight like savages who have acquired a knowledge of chemistry.
"Daily Express," April 27, 1915.

This atrocious method of warfare . . . this diabolical contrivance. . . . The wilful and systematic attempt to choke and poison our soldiers can have but one effect upon the British peoples and upon all the non-German peoples of the earth. It will deepen our indignation and our resolution, and it will fill all races with a horror of the German name.
" The Times," April 29, 1915.

But it turned out that the Germans had not been the first to use poison gas. M. Turpin's discoveries in poison explosives had been advertised in the French Press before this date, and the French War Ministry's official instructions with regard to the use of gas hand-grenades had been issued in the autumn of 1914.

In May 1915 Colonel Maude wrote in *Land and Water* :

All shells, all fires, all mining charges, give out asphyxiating gases, and from some shells the fumes are poisonous. The use of these has been discussed for years, because the explosive that liberates the deadly gas is said to possess a quite unusual power ; but the reason why many of these types were not adopted was because they were considered too dangerous for our gunners to transport and handle, not that when they burst they would have poisoned the enemy. At this time this quality of deadliness was defended on the ground of humanity, as the death inflicted would be absolutely certain and painless, and hence there would be no wounded. In any case, at the beginning of this war it was stated in all the French papers that the difficulty of handling these shells had been overcome, and that they had been employed on certain sectors of the French front with admirable results. When the time comes to defend their use, shall we really have the effrontery to claim for our shells that they poison but do not asphyxiate? Moreover, is not poisoning also covered by the Hague Convention? In spirit it undoubtedly is; but as I have not the text at hand to refer to, it may possibly leave a loophole on this question, through which our international lawyers might escape.

Subsequently, of course, we adopted gas warfare and perfected it.

MR. BILLING : Is it not a fact . . . that we have a better gas and a better protection and that now the Huns are squealing?

MR. BONAR LAW : I wish I were as sure of that as the Honourable Member.

House of Commons, February 25, 1918.

Their (the British and French) gas masks to-day are more efficient than the German; their gas is better and is better used.

" Daily Mail," February 25, 1918.

The Allies vied with one another in the production of poison gas, and the following article, by Mr. Ed. Berwick, an American, shows the extent to which it had reached before the end.

There were sixty-three different kinds of poison gas used before the war ended, and in November 1918 our chemical warfare service (established in June of that year) was engaged in sixty-five "major research problems," including eight gases more deadly than any used up to that date. . . . One kind rendered the soil barren for seven years, and a few drops on a tree-trunk causes it to "wither in an hour." Our arsenal at Edgewood, Maryland, and its tributaries was turning out 810 tons weekly against 385 tons by France, 410 tons Britain, and only 210 Germany.

It was almost ready to increase its output to 3,000 tons a week. . . . Congress had appropriated 100,000,000 dollars for this chemical warfare service and allotted 48,000 men for its use. The armistice rendered needless both allotment and appropriation in such magnitude.

Foreign Affairs, July 1922.

Poison gas of incredible malignity, against which only a secret mask (which the Germans could not obtain in time) was proof, would have stifled all resistance and paralysed all life on the hostile front subject to attack.

"*What War in* 1919 *would have Meant,*" *by Mr. Winston Churchill,* "*Nash's Pall Mall Magazine,*" *September* 1924.

Since the war, research and experiments have continued, and Great Britain is now said to lead the way in this "atrocious method of warfare," "this diabolical contrivance," the weapon of "savages."

Submarine warfare produced the same effect.

Germany cannot be allowed to adopt a system of open piracy and murder.

Mr. Churchill, House of Commons, February 15, 1915.

To-day for the first time in history one of the Great Powers in Europe proposes to engage in the systematic conduct of maritime war by means hitherto condemned by all nations as piratical.

"*The Times,*" *February* 18, 1915.

It is unnecessary to multiply the instances of violent and righteous indignation on the part of the Press and individuals.   But long before this event the other side of the question had been put by no less a person than Sir Percy Scott, who, writing in reply to Lord Sydenham in *The Times* on July 16, 1914, that is, before the outbreak of war, gave the following quotation from a letter written by a foreign naval officer, and his comment on it:

If we went to war with an insular country depending for its food supplies from overseas, it would be our business to stop that supply.   On the declaration of war we should notify the enemy that she should warn those of her merchant ships coming home not to approach the island, as we were establishing a blockade of mines and submarines.

Similarly we should notify all neutrals that such a blockade had been established, and that if any of their vessels approached the island they would be liable to destruction either by mines or submarines, and therefore would do so at their own risk.

Commentary furnished by Sir Percy Scott :

Such a proclamation would, in my opinion, be perfectly in order, and once it had been made, if any British or neutral ships disregarded it, they could not be held to be engaged in the peaceful avocations referred to by Lord Sydenham, and, if they were sunk in the attempt, it could not be described as a relapse into savagery or piracy in its blackest form.   If Lord Sydenham will look up the accounts of what usually happened to the blockade-runners into Charleston during the Civil War in America, I think he will find that the blockading cruisers seldom had any scruples about firing into the vessels they were chasing or driving them ashore, and even peppering them, when stranded, with grape and shell.   The mine and the submarine torpedo will be newer deterrents.

In one of his characteristically facetious letters (addressed to Admiral Tirpitz on his resignation, March 29, 1916), Lord Fisher wrote :

I don't blame you for the submarine business. I'd have done the same myself, only our idiots in England wouldn't believe it when I told 'em.

There was the same outburst over air-raids. We were given the impression that the Huns were the first to rain down death from the sky. But among the lantern lectures for propaganda purposes given in 1918 by the National War Service Committee, there were slides illustrating bomb-dropping on German towns. The printed synopsis of one of these slides ran :

These early raids by R.N.A.S. were the first examples of bomb-dropping attacks from the air in any war, and the pity is that we had not enough aeroplanes at the beginning of the war.

Lord Montagu said in the House of Lords in July 1917 that

it was absolute humbug to talk of London being an un-defended city. The Germans had a perfect right to raid London. London was defended by guns and aeroplanes, and it was the chief centre of the production of munitions. We were therefore but deluding ourselves in talking about London being an undefended city, and about the Germans in attacking it being guilty of an act unworthy of a civilized nation. That might be an unpopular thing to say at the moment, but it was the actual fact of the situation. The right line for the Government to take was to say to the civil population : " This is a war of nations, and not alone of armies, and you must endeavour to bear the casualties you suffer in the same way as the French and Belgian civil populations are bearing the casualties incidental to this kind of warfare.

Raids on German towns such as Karlsruhe were undertaken by the Allies, and all talk of inhumanity was dropped.

Who does not remember the fierce indignation in Great Britain at the news that the Germans had sunk to such unspeakable depths as to use poisonous gases? The British censors gladly passed the most horrifying details as to the suffering caused by this new method of torture. Soon the London censor forbade further reference of any kind to the use of gas, which meant, of course, that England was going to do a little poisoning on her own account. To-day the use of gas by the British is hailed, not only without shame, but with joyous satisfaction. Like the Allied killing of innocent women and children in German towns by their fliers, it shows again how rapidly one's ideals go by the board in war.

"*New York Evening Post*," *June* 30, 1916.

XXVII

OTHER LIES

With such profusion was falsehood sown that it would be impossible at this already distant date to gather in the whole crop. A mere assertion, even from a private individual, was often enough to set the ball rolling. The Press was only too grateful for any suggestion which might release another flood of lies, and the Government, when it was not concerned with its own subterfuges, was always ready, by disowning responsibility, to avoid direct denial of popular lies.

A few cases of some less important and some more ridiculous tales may be given.

The Governess.

Almost every foreign governess or waiter in the country was under grave suspicion, and numberless were the stories invented about them. The best edition of the governess story is given by Sir Basil Thomson: [1]

A classic version was that the governess was missing from the midday meal, and that when the family came to open her trunks, they discovered under a false bottom a store of high-explosive bombs. Everyone who told this story knew the woman's employer; some had even seen the governess herself in happier days: "Such a nice, quiet person, so fond of the children; but now one comes to think of it, there was something in her face, impossible to describe, but a something."

---

[1] *Queer People*, by Sir Basil Thomson.

✸ THE WAITER.

A Swiss waiter who had drawn on a menu-card a plan of the tables in the hotel dining-room where he was in charge was actually brought in hot haste to Scotland Yard on the urgent representations of a visitor to the hotel, who was convinced that the plan was of military importance.

A German servant girl at Bearsden, near Glasgow, with a trunk full of plans and photographs, was another fabrication.

ENAMELLED ADVERTISEMENTS.

There was a report that enamelled iron advertisements for " Maggi soup," which were attached to hoardings in Belgium, were unscrewed by German officers in order that they might read the information about local resources which was painted in German on the back by spies who had preceded them. Whether this was true or not, it was generally accepted, and screwdriver parties were formed in the London suburbs for the examination of the backs of enamelled advertisements.

CONCRETE PLATFORMS.

The emplacements laid down for guns at Maubeuge, made in the shape of tennis-courts, led to an amazingly widespread belief that all hard courts, paved back gardens, or concrete roofs were designed for this purpose. Anyone who possessed one of these came under suspicion, not only in the British Isles but in America, and the scare actually spread to California.

The *Bystander* had a cartoon in March 1915 of Bernhardi writing his books, a sword in his teeth and a revolver in his left hand, on the wall a plan labelled " proposed concrete bed at Golders Green."

THE TUBES.

The Tube as a refuge from Zeppelin raids naturally came in for attention. Sir Basil Thomson gives one of the forms of an invention in this connection.

An English nurse had brought a German officer back from death's door. In a burst of gratitude, he said, at parting, " I must not tell you more, but beware of the Tubes in April (1915)." As time wore on the date was shifted forward month by month. We took the trouble to trace this story from mouth to mouth until we reached the second mistress in a London boarding-school. She declared that she had heard it from the charwoman who cleaned the school, but that lady stoutly denied she had ever told so ridiculous a story.

BOMBING OF HOSPITALS.

In May 1918 the Press was filled with articles of the most violent indignation at the deliberate bombing of hospitals by the Germans. *The Times* (May 24, 1918), said : " It was on a par with all the abominations that have caused the German name to stink in the nostrils of humanity since the war began, and will cause it to stink while memory endures," and recommended, after they had been vanquished, " ostracism from the society of civilized nations." There was a *Punch* cartoon, and the rest of the Press yelled. The soldiers, however, as usual, did not indulge in hysterics, and explained the matter of the bombing of the hospitals at Etaples, after which the following appeared in a leader published by the *Manchester Guardian*.

Towards the end of last month and the beginning of this public opinion here—and, for the matter of that, we imagine in most other countries too—was horrified by messages from correspondents in France who described the deliberate bombing of British hospitals by German airmen. In one case the correspondent asserted categorically that there could have been no mistake; the hospitals, and not anything of military value, were the objects at whose destruction the raiders aimed. Well might such news cause even a fiercer fire of indignation than now burns against the Germans, since inhumanity could reach no lower depth than an attack on the sick and wounded and those who minister to them. There was no apparent room to doubt the accuracy of these reports, for there is a censorship in the field which not only prevents the correspondent from saying anything that it disapproves, but can overtake an error if by some mischance he has fallen, as he may easily do, into inaccuracy. So long, then, as these reports arrived and went uncorrected, it was right to suppose that they represented the facts. But we believe it is the view of the military authorities that there is no sufficient evidence to show that these were deliberate attacks on hospitals. The military view is that hospitals must sometimes, on both sides of the front, be placed near objects of military importance, such as railways or camps or ammunition dumps, and that in a night raid hospitals run the risk of being hit when the military objects round them are attacked. But if this is the authoritative military view, how comes it that correspondents were allowed to send misleading messages to this country, or that when messages had been sent, steps were not taken to remove the impression they had caused? Our case against the Germans is strong enough in all conscience, and thoroughly established. We can afford to do justice even to them, and we ought to do no less.

" Manchester Guardian," June 15, 1918.

The constant assertion that on no occasion were hospital ships used for the carrying of any war material or soldiers was contrary to fact.

THE CROWN PRINCE.

The German Crown Prince, when he was not dead, was always represented as stealing valuables from

French châteaux. The following is a sample of what it was thought necessary to write on this subject :

> The Crown Prince of Prussia may yet be immortalized as a prince among burglars and a burglar among princes ! . . . Germany makes war in a manner that would have commended itself to Bill Sikes, and the Kaiser's eldest son, in his eagerness to secure the " swag," has merited the right to be considered an imperial Fagin. . . . This modern Germany, whose spirit is epitomized in the Crown Prince, fights like a valiant blackguard. It will die like a hero, but it will murder like an apache and will steal like a mean pickpocket.
> *Thefts by the Crown Prince*, " *Daily Express*," November 1, 1914.

An article appeared in *La Nouvelle Revue* in 1915, written by an Irish lady whose friend had witnessed a secret ceremony at Menin at which " the German Crown Prince was crowned King of Belgium in the market-place." This was reproduced in the English Press.

TUBERCULOSIS GERMS.

The Germans were accused of having inoculated French prisoners with tuberculosis germs. So emphatic was this assertion that a question was asked in Parliament on the subject on April 24, 1917. The Government, however, disclaimed having any information on the subject, and the story was dropped.

THE PATRIOTIC LIAR.

The method of the patriotic liar can be illustrated by the case of a clergyman, who informed the Manchester Geographical Society on October 7, 1914: " You will hear only one hundredth part of the actual atrocities this war has produced. The civilized world could not stand the truth. It will never hear it. There are,

up and down England to-day, scores—I am under-
stating the number—of Belgian girls who have had
their hands cut off. That is nothing to what we could
tell you." Later in the same month the reverend
gentleman wrote to the *Daily News*, asking, " Will
anyone who has actually *seen* such cases here in England
send me full particulars ? " He had made his statement
first and was endeavouring to get his evidence afterwards.

MINERS BURIED ALIVE.

On August 29th the *Daily Citizen* of Glasgow had
a paragraph headed " Miners Buried Alive ! Enemy
Block Shafts of Belgian Pits." On December 1st the
Daily Citizen (without heading the paragraph) gave the
statement of M. Lombard (General Secretary of the
Belgian Miners) to the Executive of the Miners' Federa-
tion of Great Britain, in which he " denied that there
was any truth in the rumour circulated so freely in this
country that the Germans had shut up the pit mouths in
various places, thus suffocating miners underground."

WAR NEWS FOR THE U.S.A.

A former agent of the Standard Oil Company, living
at Crieff, Scotland, supplied " war news " to the U.S.A.
The *Strathearn Herald*, in December 1914, gave some
samples. There was, of course, the handless Belgian
baby who had arrived in Glasgow.

Over a hundred Germans were found with cages full of
homing pigeons in Glasgow and Edinburgh.

But the most elaborate bit of news was that

when the British Army had to retreat in France about a
month ago, General French asked for reinforcements from

some of the French Generals, and was refused. Kitchener went over to the Continent the next day, and the only excuse was that the French troops were tired. Upon investigation, however, it was found that two of the French Generals had German wives. Kitchener ordered two of them to be shot.

A Soldier's Letter.

At a recent meeting in the North of England, an ex-service man in the audience related the following experience :

He was wounded and taken prisoner on the Western front, and for some time was in hospital in Germany. When well on the road to recovery, he learned that he was to be removed from the hospital, as beds were wanted for wounded Germans, and that he was being sent to a special camp for convalescents. In a short note to his relatives he informed them of the removal.

On returning home after the war, he was amazed to find that the local Press had obtained permission from his people to use the letter, and had woven around it an " atrocity " story telling how, when at the point of death, he had been taken from bed in order to make room for a slightly wounded German, and had been sent on a journey of very many miles to a camp, where his wounds could not possibly receive proper attention, so there was practically no chance of his recovery owing to this barbarism on the part of the Germans.

Faked German Order.

A private serving in the 24th Division relates how, in 1917, while in the Somme area, a typed copy of a translation of an alleged German order was circulated among the troops. The order required German women

to cohabit with civilians and soldiers on leave so that
there might be no shortage of children to make up
for war losses. Rewards were offered for those who
zealously carried out the order. Typed out by official
machines, the circular was posted up in the canteens.

RUSSIAN ARSENAL DESTROYED.

On September 15, 1915, in the *Evening News*, there
were large headlines :

BLOW THAT CRIPPLED RUSSIA
ONLY ARSENAL WRECKED BY VAST EXPLOSION

and there was a full description of how, through German
spies and treachery, " the Russian Woolwich had been
blown to pieces." " Ochta was the Russian Woolwich,
and much more than the Russian Woolwich. It was
the only munition factory in the whole of Russia."
It subsequently turned out that the Ochta explosion
was not at an arsenal at all, but was due to an accident
in a factory which had been temporarily turned into a
munition factory. No German spies had had anything
to do with it. It was an inconsiderable affair, and a
small paragraph with the true version was inserted in a
later issue of the paper.
Amusingly enough, in the same issue and on the very
same page, there appeared a satirical article on " The
Rumour Microbe," laughing at a man who said " That
a relative of his had a relation who had seen a Zeppelin
come down on Hampstead Heath, and a man went to
some stables and got out a number of horses, which
towed it away."
The careful perusal of the files of newspapers, British
and foreign, during these four years, would yield an

amazing harvest of falsehood.   As the public mind is always impressed by anything that appears in print, the influence of the Press in inflaming one people against the other must have been very considerable, and in many people's opinion very laudable.

XXVIII

THE MANUFACTURE OF NEWS

THE FALL OF ANTWERP.

November 1914.

When the fall of Antwerp got known, the church bells were rung (meaning in Germany).

Kölnische Zeitung.

According to the *Kölnische Zeitung*, the clergy of Antwerp were compelled to ring the church bells when the fortress was taken.

Le Matin.

According to what *Le Matin* has heard from Cologne, the Belgian priests who refused to ring the church bells when Antwerp was taken have been driven away from their places.

The Times.

According to what *The Times* has heard from Cologne via Paris, the unfortunate Belgian priests who refused to ring the church bells when Antwerp was taken have been sentenced to hard labour.

Corriére della Sera.

According to information to the *Corriére della Sera* from Cologne via London, it is confirmed that the barbaric conquerors of Antwerp punished the unfortunate Belgian priests for their heroic refusal to ring the church bells by hanging them as living clappers to the bells with their heads down.

Le Matin.

L

XXIX

WAR AIMS

As there was great uncertainty how, if victory were achieved, the spoils would be divided, it was impossible for statesmen, in the Allied nations, to be precise as to what specific aims with regard to territorial adjustments and colonial acquisitions could be laid down as desirable objects, without rousing jealousy and suspicion amongst themselves.   It became necessary therefore to announce some general high-sounding moral ideals which might give the war the character of an almost religious crusade. They were particularly unfortunate in selecting a number of cries everyone of which has proved, in the long run, to be false.

A WAR TO CRUSH MILITARISM.

Everyone knows now that militarism cannot be crushed by war.   Even if it is removed from one quarter it only grows stronger elsewhere.   Militarism can only be crushed by the growth of real democracy in an era of peace.   Only a few figures are required to show how false this cry was if it was ever believed by anyone.   The *Morning Post* was honest enough to refer to it as " this absurd talk."

THE BRITISH EMPIRE.
EXPENDITURE ON FIGHTING SERVICES.

1913–14.	1924–25.
£110,750,000	£117,525,000

While fully taking into account the fall in the value of money, which would show a slight decrease in the second figure rather than increase, no substantial reduction, which might be expected as a consequence of a war to end militarism, is in any way apparent.

For the same period the aggregate totals for the four Allied powers, France, Italy, the United States, and Japan are :

1913.	1925.
£194,380,625	£244,864,477

Since the war, that is to say, from 1918 to 1926, Great Britain has spent over £1,300,000,000 on armaments.   To have said therefore that the war would crush militarism, was the most extravagant and foolish of all speculations.   It would be an insult to the intelligence of any of the statesmen to suggest that they ever for a moment believed it would be true.

A WAR TO DEFEND SMALL NATIONALITIES.

The ultimatum to Serbia and the infringement of Belgian neutrality led to the widespread cry that we were fighting " for the rights of small nationalities."

It means next that room must be found and kept for the independent existence and free development of the smaller nationalities, each with a corporate consciousness of its own. *Mr. Asquith on War Aims, Dublin, September* 26, 1914.

There were a host of other declarations from responsible Ministers of a similar character.

But this was no more true than any of the other cries.   Apart from the minorities placed under alien rule by frontier delimitations drawn for strategic purposes and not according to race or nationality, Montenegro was wiped off the map by the Peace Treaties, although the restoration of Montenegro was specially mentioned by the Prime Minister on January 5, 1918 (National War Aims pamphlet No. 33), the British occupation of Egypt continues, the Syrians have been subjected to severe repression by the French (the bombing of Damascus), the attempt of the Riffs at securing independence led to their being blotted out, Nicaragua and Panama are being subjected to the political domination of the United States, and other instances might be given in which the struggle of "small nationalities" is simply regarded as a revolutionary or subversive move. There may be good political reasons for the instances given in the eyes of the Great Powers, but the endeavour to persuade the people that we were fighting for small nationalities was the purest hypocrisy.

A War to Make the World Safe for Democracy.

The absurdity of this meaningless cry on the part of the Allies, amongst whom was Czarist Russia, is obvious. Its insincerity is proved by results. There is now the most ruthless dictatorship ever established in Italy; an imitation of it in Spain; a veiled dictatorship in Poland; a series of attempted dictatorships in Greece; something which approaches near to a dictatorship in Hungary; Turkey and Persia are both dominated by individuals with almost sovereign prerogatives, and the Soviet system is a form of dictatorship. In fact, except in Great Britain, the United States, the Scandinavian countries, Belgium, Holland, and Switzerland, parliamentary government has been in grave danger where it has not been entirely superseded.

A War to End War.

This was hardly an original cry. It has been uttered in previous wars, although every schoolboy knows that war breeds war.

We have long been deceived by the false counsels of politicians and sentimentalists who are even now pretending that this is a war that will end war. War will never end as long as human nature continues to be human nature.

"Morning Post," October 20, 1915.

So far as the Great War is concerned, the *Morning Post* seems to be correct up to date. Since 1918 fighting has never ceased in the world. There has been war on the part of the Allies against Russia, war between Turkey and Greece, the Black and Tan exploits in Ireland, the armed occupation of the Ruhr, war of France and Spain against the Riffs, war of France against the Syrians, military action on the part of the U.S.A. in Nicaragua, fighting in Mexico, and incessant war in China.

No Territory for Great Britain.

The statement that whatever we were fighting for we desired no fresh territory was frequently made. Considering that the British Empire comprised over thirteen million square miles of the earth's surface in 1914, the statement was accepted as wise and sensible. A few of the chief declarations on the subject may be given.

We have no desire to add to our Imperial burdens either in area or in responsibility.

Mr. Asquith, October 1914.

Our direct and selfish interests are small.

Mr. Asquith, November 1914.

We are not fighting for territory.

Mr. Bonar Law, December 1916.

We are not fighting a war of conquest.

Mr. Lloyd George, February 1917.

Such a victory as will give not aggrandizement of territory nor any extension of our Empire.

Mr. Long, February 1917.

So much for the protestations for public consumption. Now as to the facts with regard to what "fell to us" when it was all over.

	Square Miles.
Egypt, formerly under Turkish suzerainty, became part of the British Empire	350,000
Cyprus, formerly under Turkish suzerainty, became part of the British Empire	3,584
German South-West Africa, mandate held by the Union of South Africa	322,450
German East Africa, mandate held by Great Britain	384,180
Togoland and Cameroons, divided between Great Britain and France (say half)	112,415
Samoa, mandate held by New Zealand	1,050
German New Guinea and Island south of Equator, mandate held by Australia	90,000
Palestine, mandate held by Great Britain	9,000
Mesopotamia (Iraq), mandate held by Great Britain	143,250
Total in square miles	1,415,929

This is not a bad total of "conquest" "territory," "addition to Imperial burdens in area and responsibility," and "extension of Empire." But surely it would have been better not to make the false declarations which inevitably bring against us the charge of hypocrisy.

XXX

FOREIGN LIES

(A) GERMANY.

THE similarity of the lines on which lying was conducted in Germany to our own in this country shows well how duping the people is a necessary adjunct of war all the world over.

Within the nation the censorship was stricter than it was here. No decent word with regard to the enemy was allowed, and the good treatment of prisoners in British camps was suppressed. The same amazing stupidity with regard to concealments was shown as in this country. But a worse mistake was made in depicting the situation up to the end in rose colour and with exaggerated optimism. The real truth as to the course of events was concealed, every enemy success was understated, the effect of American intervention was minimized, the condition of German resources exaggerated, so that when the final catastrophe came, many people were taken by surprise. In this connection the Germans have got a stronger indictment against their authorities than we have. Cautions and warnings were not omitted in this country.

The Press Bureau (Pressekonferenz) was presided over by a soldier. Casualties were, so far as possible, concealed. On November 15, 1914, the Pressekonferenz stated there were a few hundred casualties, while the official list contained at the time 55,000 names. One of the members of the Pressekonferenz echoed our War

Office circular [1] when he said, on one occasion, in dealing with a false official report : " It is not so much the accuracy of the news as its effect that matters." [2]

The Turks were embarrassing allies. The massacres of Armenians had to be concealed, although attempts were made in some papers to defend them.

Our poet-writers and professors had their exact counterparts in Germany and gave orthodox "patriotism " an intellectual and literary tone.

Abroad, German lying was not very skilful. It was either too subtle or too clumsy. They had a wide field to cover with so many nations against them. "Encirclement " was the chief cry and, in the case of Russia and France, aggression.

In October 1914 Prince Rupprecht of Bavaria declared that England's ambition " for years had been turned to surround us with a ring of enemies in order to strangle us " (uns mit einem Ring von Feinden zu umgeben um uns zu erdrosseln), and there were many similar declarations.

With regard to the deliberate policy of encirclement, so far as Great Britain is concerned, Herr Rudolf Kircher remarks, in his book *Engländer* (1926) :

Grey's personality is the living proof that a policy of encirclement as a war aim, as was imagined in Germany, never existed. All these were fantastic suppositions, as fantastic as the idea that the German people were ripe and ready for an attack and struggle for world supremacy.

The German Government, like all the other Governments, was blameless and at the mercy of the machinations of enemy Governments. They had no chief Monster to depict as the Allies had, but only a number

---

[1] See page 20.   [2] *Die grosse Zeit der Lüge*, Hellmut v. Gerlach.

of not very distinguished statesmen. In the early days of panic they started with "a military report" that "French aviators had dropped bombs in the vicinity of Nuremberg" on August 3, 1914, and flaming headlines appeared in the newspapers. But the Prussian Minister at Munich telegraphed to Berlin that there was "no evidence of dropping of bombs and still less, naturally, that the aviators were French" (Kautsky documents, No. 758). At the same time there was a report from the Governor of Düsseldorf that "eighty French officers in the uniform of Prussian officers, in twelve automobiles, had made a vain attempt to cross the frontier at Walbeck." Both these reports were telegraphed by Herr Jagow, the Minister of Foreign Affairs, to the Ministers at Brussels and The Hague, to be brought to the attention of the Governments as a violation of international law. Both were no doubt believed, but neither of them had any foundation. On the other hand, there were several instances of the violation of French territory by German frontier patrols before August 3, 1914.

Apart from the absurdities of "Gott strafe England" and "the Hymn of Hate," Great Britain was naturally singled out for special attention. On September 3, 1914, the *Frankfurter Zeitung* printed a speech by Mr. John Burns which was purely imaginary. In October there appeared in the New York American an interview with a "highly placed representative of the British Government" which was proved to be entirely false. Aeroplanes were used to drop on French trenches and billets picture-postcards of ruined French churches with the legend on them, "Wrecked by the English." There were the usual exaggerated reports and startling statements as to what was going on in enemy countries, despair, demoralization and panic, accusations of abuse of the " white flag," specially against British troops, and other " necessary " war lies.

Neutral countries, of course, received propaganda from both sides. There was a German film depicting German soldiers feeding Belgian and French children, and English prisoners grinning with delight as they worked under the stern eyes of the Prussian soldiers.

On November 25, 1914, the *Norddeutsche Allgemeine Zeitung* published in facsimile a translation of a report written by General Ducarne to the Belgian War Minister on April 10, 1906, recording the visit of Colonel Barnardiston with regard to the dispatch of the Expeditionary Force in the event of war between Germany and France. In the translation which was reproduced in other newspapers without the facsimile there were three mistakes.

(*a*) An interpolation, which was an integral part of the text, ran as follows : " L'entrée des Anglais en Belgique ne se ferait qu'après la violation de notre neutralité par l'Allemagne." (The entry of the British into Belgium will only take place after the violation of our neutrality by Germany.) This was represented as a marginal note and given in French, so that many readers would not understand it.

(*b*) In the passage : " He (Colonel Barnardiston) emphasized that our conversation must be absolutely confidential," the word " conversation " was translated by *Abkommen*, as if it were " convention."

(*c*) The final date in French, " Fin Septembre 1906," was translated " Abgeschlossen September 1906," i.e. " concluded," giving the impression of " a convention " having been " concluded."

The mistakes, each taken separately, might have been

errors of carelessness, but taken all three together,
undoubtedly point to a deliberate attempt at falsification.

In the early months of the war the Wolff Bureau
circulated a report in the papers: " To-day a French
doctor, assisted by two French officers in disguise,
attempted to infect a well at Metz with plague and
cholera bacillus ; the criminals were caught and shot."
An official *démenti* of this story was subsequently issued.

The greatest tunnel in Germany, at Cochen, on the
frontier, was reported to have been destroyed by an
innkeeper, Nicolai, of Cochen, and his son, both of
whom were shot. The *Rheinish-Westfälische Zeitung*
stated that after careful investigation it was discovered
that Nicolai was a naturalized German, French by
birth, and it was a matter for congratulation that the
criminal was not a genuine German. The following
day the sub-Prefect of Cochen announced that there
was not a word of truth in the supposed plot ; Nicolai
was alive and a highly respected citizen, whilst his
son was serving in a Prussian regiment.

Atrocity lies abounded in Germany just as in this
country. Gouging out of eyes there seems to have been
as great a favourite as the Belgian babies without hands
here.

In September 1914 a lady of Cologne was informed
that a whole room was given up in a hospital at Aix-la-
Chapelle to wounded soldiers who had had their eyes
gouged out in Belgium. On inquiry, a leading doctor at
Aix-la-Chapelle declared there was no such room and
no single case of the sort had been observed. But the
story wandered from Aix-la-Chapelle to Bonn, where
again the chief doctor of the hospitals had to deny it.
Then it travelled to Sigmaringen. The *Weser Zeitung*
in Bremen took it up and wrote in a similar way about

a hospital in Berlin. This was denied by the Kom-
mandatur der Residenz. It reached its climax when it
was reported that a small boy of ten had seen "a whole
bucketful of soldiers' eyes" (ein ganzer Eimer voll
Soldaten-augen).

Die Zeit in Bild (January 12, No. 38) gave circumstantial accounts of a priest who wore a chain round
his neck made up of rings taken from fingers he had
cut off.

An official report from Luttich, where this was
supposed to have happened, stated there was no such
case.

In the *Kölnische Volkszeitung*, September 15, 1914, it
was related how a company of German soldiers were
marching through a Belgian village when the priest,
who stood before the door of the church, invited the
captain to come in with his soldiers, "for it was
good," he said, "even in these dark times, to think of
God (da es doch in dieser schweren Zeit gut sei auch
an den lieben Gott zu denken). The captain accepted
the invitation. A machine gun was concealed behind
the altar. When the church was full the machine gun
was unmasked and the whole company shot down.

Such stories as these [1] arose chiefly from anti-Catholic
bias. Priests were accused of harbouring French
soldiers in their houses, but no case was proved. An
incident of which many and varied versions were given
was that of Demange, priest of Lagarde. He was said to
have betrayed the position of the German troops to the
enemy, to have put a machine gun in the tower of his
church with which to shoot down Germans. He was
reported to have been shot, and his body pierced by
thirty bayonet wounds was seen before the church door

[1] See *Der Lügengeist in Völkerkrieg*, by Bernard Duhr.

of Lagarde. Not only was the whole thing an invention, but it turned out, from official information, that Demange, who was alive, had behaved with heroism in resisting the enemy, and had been praised by German officers.

The variations of the story and its exposure as a falsehood appeared in the *Frankfürter Zeitung* (September 18, 1914) and the *Kölnische Volkszeitung* (October 11, 1914).

On August 31, 1914, the *Berliner Lokalanzeiger* reported that a nurse in Amsterdam had heard from a German officer how, after Löwen had been occupied, all was quiet. But later the bodies of fifty German soldiers, shot by the monks, were found in the cellar of the monastery. The inmates were thereupon arrested and the Superior shot.

This story was widely circulated, and as it was likely to embitter religious feeling General von Bissing issued a complete denial of the report and an order that it should not be circulated in the Press (Münster, September 6, 1914). Nevertheless the story has been incorporated in several German books on the war.

In September 1914 Sergeant (Unteroffizier) Adolf Schmidt related, in a letter to his parents, how he and his troop had been invited by a French priest to have some coffee. Being suspicious, he called a doctor to examine the coffee, and found it had strychnine mixed with it. The priest and his cook were shot the next morning (*Schwarzwälder Chronik*, September 18, 1914).

The whole story proved to be an invention of the sergeant, who retracted it.

In April 1915 the *Vossische Zeitung* reported the invasion of Egypt by the Senussi with an army of 70,000 men. This invention was reproduced in the

Corriére della Sera in Italy and denied by the British Embassy.

A letter (August 26, 1914) to the *Hamburger Fremden-blatt* related how the Belgians supplied the German troops with cigars filled with gunpowder, which blinded them when they lit them. Another letter to the *Berliner Tageblatt* (August 26th) reported that the Belgians filled the letters of the Germans with narcotic powder.

On January 23, 1915, the *Kölnische Zeitung* gave the most gruesome description, by an eye-witness, of a scene on the Eastern front in which a boy of twelve years old had been secured to a table by nails driven through each of his fingers. Judge Rosenberg, of Essen, took the matter up and asked the name of the place where this had happened. After delay and evasions and considerable difficulty in discovering the author of the tale, he ascertained that it had taken place at Prostken. Accordingly he wrote to the authorities there, and received a reply on September 14, 1916, to the effect that nothing was known of any such incident in the district.

That there were incidents of cruelty and barbarity on the Eastern front there can be no doubt. But these were exaggerated until wholesale accusations were made against the Russians for habitually cutting off men's arms and legs and women's breasts.

Both on the East and West, atrocity stories were circulated without the names of place or person.

The following is an instance of the kind of story which the German public was made to accept as typical of the methods of their enemies.

On October 29, 1915, the *Kölnische Volkszeitung* described the following incident :

In consequence of the proclamation of the Holy War, a number of British Askari of Mohammedan religion refused to fight against the Germans of East Africa; thereupon these 112 " rebels " were handcuffed and thrashed and taken to Nairobi, where they were condemned by court martial to be hanged. But a few days later, instead of hanging them, a new order was given, according to which the condemned men were to be used as living targets for the black recruits in their rifle practice. One morning in November of last year ten of these prisoners were taken to a place south of Nairobi, where some British Askaris were in camp. The condemned men had first of all to dig a huge pit, where they were afterwards to be buried. They were then bound, hand and foot, gagged, and placed in the bushes, tall grass or on trees, so that only a small part of their bodies was visible. English officers gave the instructions in shooting. At a distance of from 100 to 300 paces the recruits shot at their living targets. This practice lasted the whole morning and afternoon, and by the evening two men were found to be dead, and the others, who were terribly wounded, were then killed. The bodies were then thrown into the pit. This shooting practice was continued daily until all the condemned men were killed.

An Englishman who was in Berlin in the early days of the war heard, at the International Trade Union headquarters, continual discussions as to the possibility of reaching and attacking the British coast. It was argued that such an attack would shatter the prestige of Great Britain. The Englishman maintained that it would only greatly assist recruiting.

When the actual bombardment of Hartlepool, Scarborough, and Whitby took place, the morning Press gave large type to the event. " Fortified Towns of Hartlepool, Whitby, and Scarborough Bombarded." Then followed the Wolff Telegraph Bureau description of the nature of the fortifications on the hill at Scarborough and again at Whitby. The text carried the implication that it was because these were well-known fortified towns that they had been selected for bombardment. The matter was discussed on the day the newspaper was published, and the German Trade Unionists pointed again and again to the evidence in the Press of the military nature of these three towns. The Englishman accurately described Hartlepool and Scarborough as favourite holiday resorts of British children and Whitby as a place of pilgrimage for visitors both from England and America. But he made no impression. They were greatly annoyed and preferred their own lie, which was universally accepted in Germany. It will be remembered that the *Daily Mail* replied with a row of photographs of babies.

A lie exposed by no less a person than the Foreign Secretary must certainly be recorded. Sir Edward Grey, speaking on May 25, 1916, in the House of Commons, referred to a statement of the German Chancellor (Herr von Bethmann-Hollweg) in the following terms :

I did find one new thing in the statement of the German Chancellor with regard to the terms of peace. That is the statement as to what the attitude of the British Government was in the time of diplomatic difficulty about Bosnia. That statement is untrue so far as we are concerned. The charge that our attitude was bellicose about the negotiations concerning Bosnia is a first-class lie. The idea that we attempted to urge Russia to war and that we said that this country would be ready to go to war about Bosnia is directly contrary to the truth.

(B) FRANCE.

Whatever criticisms may be made of the French, we can never accuse them of being hypocrites. They realized the great importance of " propaganda " and went to work with a will. They are neither ashamed of the fact nor attempt to conceal it. We always mixed our lies up with righteous indignation and high morality, and tried to make them as statesmanlike and genteel as possibie, although the *Kadaver* story was perhaps the most atrocious as well as the most successful lie in the war. The French authorities were delighted with it, and an English war correspondent has related how the French correspondents were made to send in reports of the corpse factory over their own signatures.

It will be remembered that in the eventful days before August 4, 1914, the French Government declared that they showed their pacific disposition by retiring all their troops ten kilometres from the frontier—a gesture which was acclaimed here and in France as magnificent and magnanimous and heroic. The truth, however, was that the French desired to delay, as long as possible, the declaration of war so as to give full time for the preparations in Great Britain and Russia. This is how a Frenchman writes of it :

It was evident that if this order were in the least degree to compromise the success of our plans, our generals would not have tolerated it. One can say with absolute certainty that if there were any points where our troops could keep back ten kilometres from the frontier, it would be at points where it would not be inconvenient, and in the places where it would be necessary for them to be nearer they would be nearer. In fact, there were certain points where they remained on the frontier, and many, according to M. Messimy (Minister for War), where they were withdrawn only four or five kilometres. Moreover, after August 2nd, 5.30 p.m., that is, a whole day before Germany's declaration of war, the order was suppressed on the pretext that three German patrols had in the morning made an incursion into our territory.

M

Without doubt the ten-kilometre retreat was only a fool's trap specially designed to make the English believe that the French mobilization was a pacific mobilization.

M. Demartial, in " L'Évangile du Quai d'Orsay," 1926.

A good many of the lies circulated in Great Britain originated from across the channel. The French were adepts at faked photographs ; instances are given under that heading. The insinuations in their merciless caricatures also had considerable influence with those to whom pictures appeal.

Lies in France were, many of them, the same as those with which we were provided here. But their method was more extensive and thorough, as is shown by the disclosures in *Behind the Scenes of French Journalism*, by " A French Chief Editor," from the eighth chapter of which book the following extracts are taken.

. . . If you reduce the lie to a scientific system, put it on thick and heavy, with great effort and sufficient finances scatter it all over the world as the pure truth, you can deceive whole nations for a long time and drive them to slaughter for causes in which they have not the slightest interest. We have seen that sufficiently during the last war, and will see it in the next one, by which a kind providence will clumsily try to solve the problem of over-population.

We concluded immediately, and very correctly, that it is not sufficient to inflame the masses for war, and, in order to escape the accusation of the war-guilt, to represent the enemy as a dangerous disturber of the peace and the most terrible enemy of mankind.

We have not waited for Lord Northcliffe's procedure. On the spur of the moment we appreciated the great importance to enthuse public opinion for our more or less just cause. As early as three days after the outbreak of the war, Viviani promulgated a law which on the same day was passed by the House and the Senate, and which provided as the first instalment of a powerful propaganda the trifling amount of twenty-five million francs in gold for the establishment of

LA MAISON DE LA PRESSE,

a gigantic building, Francois Street 3, five stories high, without the basement, where the printing-presses are located, and the ground-floor with its large meeting hall.   A busy, lively going and coming, as in a beehive ; trucks arriving, elegant autos with pretentious-looking persons.   The two hundred rooms contain the workshops, offices, parlours, and reception-rooms, where those war-mad heroes are domiciled whose courage grows with the degree of distance from the trenches.   From the basement up to the fifth story covered with a glass roof, all is the embodiment of concentrated propaganda.   In the basement stood the machinery necessary for printing and reproduction, under the glass roof operated the photo-chemigraphic department. Its principal work consisted in making photographs and cuts of wooden figures with cut-off hands, torn-out tongues, gouged-out eyes, crushed skulls and brains laid bare.   The pictures thus made were sent as unassailable evidence of German, atrocities to all parts of the globe, where they did not fail to produce the desired effect.   In the same rooms fictitious photographs were made of bombarded French and Belgian churches, violated graves and monuments and scenes of ruin and desolation.   The staging and painting of these scenes were done by the best scene-painters of the Paris Grand Opera. . . . The Press House was the indefatigable geyser which belched forth incessantly false war reports and fictitious news from the rear and the front, the meanest and most brutal slanders of the opponents, the astonishing fictions of infamous acts attributed to them. The insidious but efficacious poison thus broadcast has misled and infected a host of well-meaning but unsophisticated people. . . . During the war the lie became a patriotic virtue.   It was forced upon us by the Government and the censor, and through the peril of losing the war considered a necessity ; besides, lying was profitable and often publicly honoured.   It would be useless to deny the success of the lie, which used the Press as the best means of an extended and rapid circulation.   The greatest efforts were made to stamp every word of the enemies as a lie and every lie of our own as absolute truth. Everything sailed under the flag of " Propaganda."

Children's education was not neglected. In *Le Matin*, November 12, 1915, there was a paragraph headed, " To Teachers."

All French schools must possess a collection of the cards "German crimes," in order to impress for ever upon the children the atrocities of the barbarians. It went on to say that an artist of note had created a dozen compositions relating to "the most striking episodes among German crimes." . . . "Teachers, subscribe to-day and place these pictures in your schools."

Press distortions were as common in France as in other countries. As early as July 25, 1914, M. Berthelot, M. Poincaré's permanent head of the Foreign Office, caused a gravely distorted account of the Pacific conversations between Bienvenu Martin and Baron Schoen to be published in the *Écho de Paris* and *Le Matin*. Public opinion can be far more easily dragooned by Government and Press in France than it can be in this country. There was, therefore, less need for subtlety, more chance for concealment, and little fear of the crudest lies not being accepted, provided they had the hall-mark of some sort of authority. Moreover, in France there is less disposition to examine the stories and statements by which they were deceived and expose their falsity now that it is all over. Nevertheless, no people is more intelligently aware of the imbecile futility of war and its senseless barbarity than the common people of France.

(c) THE UNITED STATES.

There was no richer field for propaganda than the United States of America in the first years of the war.

The Allied Powers and the Central Powers were both
hard at work competing. The German method began
by being too subtle. A wireless news agency, under
German control, gave at first the best, most authentic,
unbiased, and by far the cheapest war news, and thus
attracted a large number of subscribers and fed the
American Press. As the months passed, their news
began to be ingeniously " slanted " in favour of the
Central Powers. But they relied too much on argument. The cruder British methods were far more
successful, and intensive work was done by the British
War Mission, which (as Lord Northcliffe stated in *The
Times*, November 16, 1917) comprised 500 officials with
10,000 assistants. Atrocities, Germany's sole responsibility, the criminal Kaiser, and all the other fabrications
started in Great Britain, were worked up by American
liars with great effect. The Belgian baby without hands
was a special favourite. There was hardly a household
in which it was not discussed all over that vast continent,
and even so ridiculous a scare as the concrete platforms
for German guns was current in California. Spy
stories abounded and effective films were produced by
those who were pressing for America to come into the
war. One particularly good one dealt with the pacific
spirit which at first prevailed. Instead of deriding it,
the pacifist hero was depicted as a fine, noble figure
standing out against the excited agitation which sur-
rounded him. The incursions of a foreign army were
graphically and dramatically produced. Villages were
burned, women carried off, and various cruelties perpetrated. The representative of a foreign Power, with
an unmistakably German cast of countenance, was
depicted as a hideous villain plotting and scheming
with evil intent. There was a particularly fine " close-

up" of him, rolling his eyes with Mephistophelian cunning, in the gallery of Congress. Finally the pacifist hero, carried away by his patriotic feelings, succumbs and supports the war with enthusiasm.

After America entered into the war a number of "actual war picture" films (prepared at Hollywood) were released. An immense army of speakers and pamphleteers were employed by the Committee on Public Information, and the country was flooded with literature describing the iniquities of the Hun.

The tragedy of the sinking of the *Lusitania*, which was of course the turning-point, was distorted to the utmost limit. Atrocity stories and faked films worked more especially on the feelings of the women, so that when neutrality was abandoned and "Uncle Sam needs you" was substituted, it took very few days to bring the whole country round. Once America was in the war, all the propaganda of the Allied nations was used and further exaggerated.

Among active patriots, John R. Rathom was conspicuous with his articles in the *Providence Journal* and with his numerous lectures. During 1917 and 1918 he led the campaign against any who could be suspected of having German sympathies. His spy stories were sensational, and he was said to be coached by the British Secret Service. In February 1918 he was issuing a series of articles on "Germany's Plot Exposed," when the *New York World* discontinued them, as they were suspicious and believed that the articles were faked. In 1920 he was charged by Franklin D. Roosevelt for circulating false and defamatory libels, and in the course of examination he admitted "drawing freely on his imagination." He was finally utterly discredited, but not till after "Rathomania" had achieved considerable success during the time that it mattered.

Some lies which were little known here seem to have circulated successfully and been swallowed down in America, such as : poisoned sugar-candy dropped by German aeroplanes for children to eat ; the outraging of nuns in Belgian convents ; the clipping of a chaplain's ears by Uhlans ; and the German deification of Hindenburg by the hymn " Hindenburg ist unser Gott " (someone with insufficient knowledge of, or ear for, German having heard Luther's hymn " Ein feste Burg ist unser Gott "). Persecution of Germans and everything German was undertaken with zeal ; Wagner was unfavourably compared to Sousa, the danger of sauerkraut was emphasized and people rooted up " bachelors' buttons " from their gardens, as being a German national flower. The frenzy with which the whole propaganda was conducted in America surpassed anything we experienced here. America being a land of extremes, colour and emphasis have to reach an exceptionally high pitch before anyone takes much notice.

In October 1918, some of the lies having become too absurdly preposterous, General Pershing and the War Department of the United States authorized the publication of the following cablegram :

A St. Louis (Missouri) paper recently received here states that a sergeant, one of fifty men sent back in connection with the Liberty Loan campaign, is making speeches in which he states : " The Germans give poisoned candy to the children to eat and hand-grenades for them to play with. They show glee at the children's dying writhings and laugh aloud when the grenades explode. I saw one American boy, about seventeen years old, who had been captured by the Germans, come back to our trenches. He had cotton in and about his ears. I asked someone what the cotton was for.

" ' The Germans cut off his ears and sent him back to tell us they want to fight men,' was the answer. ' They feed Americans on tuberculosis germs.' "

As there is no foundation whatever in fact for such statements, based on any experience we have had, I recommend that this sergeant, if the statements quoted above were made by him, be immediately returned for duty and that the statements be contradicted.

PERSHING.

The American version of the crucifixion story [1] arose from the following statement of an American soldier :

It was on October 23, 1918, that our detachment, the Fifth Marines, Second Division, entered Suippes, situated north of Châlons and west of the Argonnes Forest, the village having just been evacuated by the Germans. There we found a naked girl nailed to a barn door. In addition about half of the coffins in the village churchyard had been torn from the graves and been opened, apparently with the idea of despoiling them.

When the soldier was pressed to give more precise details, he referred to the number of the Pittsburg *Sunday Post* of February 2, 1919, in which a description of the alleged incident, accompanied by drawings—not photographs—was given.

The matter having been referred to the German State Archives, it was stated, on September 27, 1924 :

During the year 1918 no Germans were in Suippes, situated on the Suippes and north-east of Châlons. The German front, especially in October 1918, ran north of Souain. That village was in possession of the French and the village of Suippes lies seven kilometres behind to the south.

---

[1] See page 91.

A Catholic clergyman in Suippes, replying to an inquiry, dated February 18, 1925, answered :

Your American soldier could not have seen that a young girl had been crucified, for there is nothing whatever known here about this tale. That graves have been despoiled is possible, but not in the cemetery of Suippes.

In spite of the denial of the story by General March at Washington, it was introduced as the basis of a war propaganda drama which had the blessing of President Wilson.[1]

Hideous cruelties, attributed to German submarine commanders, were also widely circulated. In April 1923 Admiral Sims stated, in the *New York Tribune* :

There exists no authentic report of cruelties ever having been committed by the commander or the crew of a German submarine.

The Press reports about cruelties were only meant for propaganda purposes.

Traces of the deluge of falsehood still linger to-day among the more ignorant sections of the population. But far greater is the resentment of the disillusioned, who recognize now the quagmire of falsehood from which the whole war-fever emanated.

Mr. Kirby Page sums up the activities of the Committee of Public Information :

An examination of all this propaganda reveals the exaggerations and misrepresentations to which the American public was subjected. . . . Every Government systematically planned to deceive its own people, and a rigid censorship prevailed everywhere.

---

[1] *Duty to Civilization*, by Francis Nielson.

An interesting volume on the technique of propaganda has recently been published by Professor Lasswell, of Chicago,[1] from which the following passage may be quoted:

> So great are the psychological resistances to war in modern nations, that every war must appear to be a war of defence against a menacing, murderous aggressor. There must be no ambiguity about whom the public is to hate. The war must not be due to a world system of conducting international affairs, nor to the stupidity or malevolence of all governing classes, but to the rapacity of the enemy. Guilt and guilelessness must be assessed geographically, and all the guilt must be on the other side of the frontier. If the propagandist is to mobilize the hate of the people, he must see to it that everything is circulated which establishes the sole responsibility of the enemy.

Mr. George Creel was, in the United States, the equivalent to Lord Northcliffe. His bureau was subsidized by public money, and in the book in which he relates the amazing activities undertaken, he gives some idea of the field covered when he says: " The service cost the taxpayers $4,912,553 and earned $2,825,670.23 to be applied on expenses."[2]

(D) ITALY.

Propaganda in Italy took rather a different form. The task of the Government was to formulate a policy which would justify Italy's entry into the war and give the people expectation of definite gain. While, therefore, certain atrocity stories such as the Belgian baby without hands were circulated, it was not so much moral indignation which had to be stirred as political ambition which had to be satisfied.

[1] *Propaganda Technique in the World War*, by Harold D. Lasswell.
[2] *How We Advertised America*, by George Creel.

The future of Dalmatia was the chief point of focus. Round this the Government and the Press worked up a great campaign of falsehood.

Mazzini once said, " Istria is ours ; necessary to Italy just as the ports (*porti*) of Dalmatia are necessary to Southern Slavs."

Mazzini's name counted, and this saying was reproduced in Baron Sonino's paper, the *Giornale d'Italia* (March 11, 1918), : " Istria is ours ; necessary to Italy just as the forts (*forti*) of Dalmatia are necessary to Southern Italy."

When the falsity of this statement was pointed out in the Chamber, the reply given was that it was " a fault of the printer."

Nicolo Tomasso, a patriot of Dalmatian origin, who, till he died in 1873, was in favour of a Southern Slav confederation, was also declared, without a vestige of evidence, to be in favour of the annexation of Dalmatia by Italy.

An even more ridiculous fabrication was the publication in a Milanese newspaper of a long letter from no less a person than Abraham Lincoln, said to have been written in 1853, in which the American President assigned to Italy the entire Eastern coast of the Adriatic, as well as Corsica and Malta. Mazzini, who had been reduced to tears on reading it, had translated the letter with his own hand, and Carducci and de Amicis had expressed their admiration of it. It seemed curious that such an important document should never have been heard of before. But unfortunately Abraham Lincoln, in specifying the various territories which should be assigned to Italy, used the expressions " Venezia Tridentina " and " Venezia Giulia," designations which were used for the first time in 1866, and only came slowly into common use in subsequent years. The letter was subsequently condemned as a clumsy forgery.[1]

In 1918 an article appeared in the *Rassegna Italiana* in which a large number of famous Italians, from early Roman times onward, were quoted as being in favour of Dalmatia becoming an integral part of Italy. A painstaking research into the writings of every one of the notables mentioned produced the result that without a single exception they had all declared themselves in precisely the opposite sense.

On one occasion an impressive old man with a white beard was placed outside a meeting called in favour of the annexation of Dalmatia, who, with tears coursing down his cheeks, explained how he had been persecuted by the Dalmatians. As a matter of fact, he came from Rome.

On October 8, 1916, the *Stampa* of Turin produced a declaration from Lugano, said to have been issued by anti-Italian Yugo-Slavs, to the following effect :

The present war shows that the small States cannot have an independent life without facing great dangers to their national existence. Therefore the Yugo-Slavs recognize that it is impossible to form an independent Serbian kingdom which embraces all the Yugo-Slav territories. They desire that the unification of Slav territories should happen in triune form, namely, that the Slav countries should be included in the Austro-Hungarian monarchy, with the same rights and duties and in the same situation as Hungary.

The object of this was to incite anti-Yugo-Slav sentiment and to further Baron Sonino's policy of the retention of Austro-Hungary as a federal State. The document was a forgery, but was reproduced throughout

[1] *Dal Patto di Londra alla Pace di Roma*, Gaetano Salvemini.

Italy. *L'Unita* invited the *Stampa* to state the source of its information, but no reply was ever given.[1]

A series of telegrams was sent from the various districts of Dalmatia to the Prime Minister asking that Dalmatia might be annexed to Italy. These were all sent under the instructions of the Italian military authorities. The actual orders were subsequently discovered and published, urging that telegrams should be dispatched " expressing the keen desire of the population for annexation to Italy."

Slavophobe opinion was encouraged by every sort of device. Baron Sonino, for instance, in March 1918, declared, through his organs, that it was impossible to come to any accommodation with the Yugo-Slavs with regard to the Pact of London, because they insisted on claiming not only Dalmatia but also Pola, Trieste, and Udine. He had actually received specific assurances from M. Pashitch that these latter districts should remain in Italy's possession.

A good instance of a *volte-face* on the part of the Press under Government pressure is afforded by two extracts from the *Popolo d'Italia*, which show how the Press was used to guide public opinion and tell one people to hate or love another people.

BEFORE ROUMANIAN DECLARATION OF WAR.

People must at last cease from describing the Roumanians as our sister nation. They are not Romans at all, however much they adorn themselves with this noble appellation. They are an intermixture between the barbarous Aborigines, who were subjugated by the Romans and Slavs, Chazars, Avars, Tartars, Mongols, Huns, and Turks, and so one can easily imagine what a gang of rascals has sprung from such an origin. The Roumanian is to-day still a barbarian and an

---

[1] *La Questione dell'Adriatico*, by Maranelli and Salvemini.

individual of very inferior worth who, amid the universal ridicule of the French, apes the Parisian. He is glad enough to fish in muddy waters where none of those perils exist which he seeks to avoid as much as possible, as he has already shown in 1913.

The same newspaper wrote *after the declaration of war* :

The Roumanians have now proved in the most striking manner that they are worthy sons of the ancient Romans, from whom they, like ourselves, are descended. They are thus our nearest brethren who now, with that courage and determination which are their special qualities, are taking part in the fight of the Latin and Slav races against the German race. . . . Nothing else indeed could be expected from a people which has the honour of belonging to that Latin race which once ruled the world.

Before Italian intervention, the Press in Italy was, as may well be imagined, a mass of contradictory reports from belligerents on both sides, charges, counter-charges, atrocity accusations and denials, scares, spy stories, and every conceivable item of "news" which percolated through not only from Great Britain, France, Russia, and the Central Powers, but from the factories of more lurid and sensational reports in the Balkans.

Utterly unreliable and contradictory reports were published day by day with regard to the treatment of Cardinal Mercier. The papal authorities had to deny the existence of a radio-telegraphic station in the Vatican. Great excitement was caused by the reported existence of a secret bomb factory in an international school directed by Benedictines on the Aventine, which was proved by police investigation to be without foundation (*Corrière della Sera*, May 11, 1915). A Milan evening paper reported that German spies had been discovered and arrested by carabinieri while making maps on the railroad lines. These were found to be Milanese citizens testing a camera, and they were released at once.

Statements in the Press reporting that French willingness to treat with Germany had been prevented by British threats of reprisals (January 1915) had to be denied by the British and French Embassies in Rome.

A good instance of suppression producing falsehood can be found in a garbled report of a Parliamentary question in April 1915.

Mr. Chancellor asked the Under-Secretary for War:

Whether there was any official information showing that two hundred men belonging to one cavalry regiment became seriously ill with symptoms of blood-poisoning after inoculation against typhoid; if so, will he say whether two or three of them died; whether the two doctors who performed the inoculation were, on inquiry, found to be Austrians, tried by court martial and sentenced to penal servitude. . . .

Mr. Tennant replied:

There is no official information corresponding in any way to the statements in the first three parts of the question. No one has heard of the Austrian doctors who have been sentenced to penal servitude.

The question *without* the categorical official denial of the story was reproduced as a statement in the *Corrière della Sera*, April 18th, the object being, of course, to fan up anti-Austrian feeling.

Every report of Italy's possible adherence to one side was authoritatively denied by the other side, and various suggested bribes of territory were constantly appearing. False reports of engagements and preparations in the Balkans and elsewhere helped to keep the minds of the unfortunate Italian people in utter confusion.

*   *   *   *   *

War lies from Russia, the Balkans and other parts of the world have unfortunately been beyond the reach of a collector. While some of them may have been more lurid and fantastic, they would, if recited, hardly serve by comparison to mitigate the foulness of the streams of falsehood which found their source in the great civilized Christian nations of the world.

Is further proof needed that international war is a monster born of hypocrisy, fed on falsehood, fattened on humbug, kept alive by superstition, directed to the death and torture of millions, succeeding in no high purpose, degrading to humanity, endangering civilization and bringing forth in its travail a hideous brood of strife, conflict and war, more war? Yet statesmen still hesitate to draw the sword of their wits to destroy it.

CPSIA information can be obtained at www.ICGtesting.com
Printed in the USA
BVOW06*2129220716

456550BV00007B/10/P